Needle Felting the Animals of the NATIONAL PARKS

Sculpt 12 Wildlife Projects and Majestic Landscapes

Claudia Marie Lenart

Landauer Publishing

Needle Felting the Animals of the National Parks

Landauer Publishing, *https://landauer.foxchapelpublishing.com*, is an imprint of Fox Chapel Publishing Company, Inc.

Project Team
Editorial Director: Brian Hurley
Acquisitions Editor: Amelia Johanson
Editor: Madeline DeLuca
Designer: Wendy Reynolds
Photographer: Claudia Marie Lenart
Proofread/Index: Jean Bissell

ISBN 978-1-63981-148-9

Library of Congress Control Number: 2026932541

To learn more about the other great books from Fox Chapel Publishing, or to find a retailer near you, call toll-free at 800-457-9112 or visit us at *www.FoxChapelPublishing.com.*

We are always looking for talented authors.
To submit an idea, please send a brief inquiry to acquisitions@foxchapelpublishing.com.

Or write to:
Fox Chapel Publishing
903 Square Street
Mount Joy, PA 17552

Printed in China
First printing

MIX
Paper | Supporting responsible forestry
FSC® C147414

Contents

Introduction

Welcome to this journey into the art of creating wildlife from wool. This book represents the culmination of my years immersed in the arts—both as a needle felt artist and as a writer—and reflects my deep love for the natural world. Author Robin Wall Kimmerer reminds us that the earth has given us everything, and that we are called to give back through our gifts. Creating animals and nature scenes is my way of expressing gratitude to the great outdoors—the source of my healing, inspiration, and endless wonder.

As a young adult, I worked in national parks over three summers—Sequoia, Mount Rainier, and Yellowstone—and that experience is etched in my soul. Waking up every morning to the scent of pine trees and having encounters with bears, moose, and eagles on a regular basis is unforgettable. I continue to visit national parks when possible and keep a close relationship with the outdoors through hiking and gardening.

The projects in this book include the wildlife that resides in the arctic, the mountains, and the prairies, and they range from very easy beginner projects to more advanced. The chapter on techniques is the key to the art of needle felting animals. Delving into this chapter first and practicing will speed up your path to becoming skilled at this craft.

I took the long way to becoming a wildlife artist and my art, along with this instructional book, truly are the culmination of my skills and interests. As a child, I loved to draw and I enjoyed drawing animals—especially horses. My mom taught me how to sew, knit, crochet, and embroider. I didn't like to follow patterns, so I would just figure out how to make clothes for my dolls and design my own embroidered scenes. In college, I painted landscapes with watercolor and later became interested in colored-pencil drawing. When my son was young, I crocheted little finger puppets from natural yarn like mohair and alpaca. At that time, I wondered how I could make more realistic animals. Several years later, I discovered needle felting while browsing the Internet. Inspired by the beauty others brought to life through needle felting, I knew I had discovered my true calling.

I didn't know where to begin, so I picked up a book with some very basic instructions. From there, I taught myself how to needle felt. When I was laid off from my job as a community journalist, I decided to throw myself full time into needle felting. Having a shop on Etsy and receiving regular orders and custom orders made me continually improve my skills. I continue to learn to this day.

I hope this book not only teaches you and sparks your creativity, but also inspires you to connect with, protect, and spend time in wild landscapes and the national parks.

Supplies

When I discovered needle felting some 12 years ago, I knew immediately that it was the art form I had been seeking. One of the biggest hills to climb, however, was understanding what type of wool and how much wool to purchase. I didn't have a good concept of what an ounce of wool looked like or what terms such as "staple length" and "roving" meant. There wasn't much information available online at the time, so I learned by trial and error. Along the way, I found many wonderful online shops that offered consistent quality, but one of the best and quickest ways to learn about wool and other natural fibers is to visit a wool store in person. I am fortunate to have one within an hour drive, and I came to relish these visits—I can actually feel the various textures and compare wool from different breeds. It is especially dreamy sampling luxury fibers like cashmere, alpaca, and yak.

Alpaca roving is a nice fiber for animal top coats.

TIP

For each project, where core wool is listed in the supplies, start with 2 oz. (56.7g). Where top wool or other colored wool is listed, start with ½ oz. (14.2g).

The variety of supplies available for needle felting keeps expanding. Inventive felters are always adding tools and more sustainable supplies, like replacing polyurethane foam felting pads with natural wool felting pads. The following pages include as comprehensive an exploration of felting supplies as possible but remember to keep an eye out for new innovations!

Wool and Fibers

Wool from shearing sheep (giving them a haircut), is the primary material used in needle felting. Other fibers can also be used for felting, including alpaca wool, mohair or cashmere from goats, and even plant fibers, such as those from bamboo. Horsehair also comes in natural hues and is used to create whiskers on animals. Depending on the source, the fibers have different staple lengths (the lengths of the individual fibers) and thicknesses, measured in microns, that affect the texture and felting uses. Wool is sheared and washed, then kept curly or carded (the fibers are combed and aligned).

When creating animals, I like to use natural, undyed fibers when possible. Other than white, wool comes in shades including black, brown, caramel, fawn, and more. Variegated wool can create a nice natural look for animals and often comes in shades such as squirrel,

TIP

For most of the animals in this book, the coat will be created with carded roving or batting. Suppliers have different names for this type of wool—Living Felt offers MC-1; Big Sky Fiber Arts has Bulky Carded Corriedale; and Felted Sky has Felter's Palette. In the supplies for each project, I refer to this wool as carded roving. Top wool can be merino or Corriedale.

deer, and bear. Big Sky Fiber Arts offers a woodland collection that includes a mix of creature-hued fiber.

Felted wool comes in squares or by the yard. Felt is used to create the form for finger puppets and as a background for wool paintings. Be sure to purchase 100 percent wool felt, not polyester.

There are three types of processed wools used in this book:

Core wool has a texture that felts together easily. It is usually higher micron wool, so it's coarse and used as the basis for most needle-felted structures. It is usually available as roving (twisted ropes of carded wool) or in batts (sheets of carded wool). Roving can easily be pulled into pieces for wrapping and is puffy compared to top wool (see below). Batt wool pulls off in larger chunks than roving. Corriedale wool (which measures 24–31 microns) is a type of core wool.

Core wool roving from Big Sky Fiber Arts (left) and top wool from Shep's Wool (right).

Top wool is carded and combed into a long rope but is not twisted like roving. The fibers are longer and straighter than in roving. Merino wool (which measures 17–22 microns) is a type of top wool. These are often finer and softer and work better to create delicate elements like hair, fur, loose fabric, or wings.

Alpaca top naturally comes in white, black, gray, and tan. It can be dyed, however, and is great for adding hair and fur to your sculptures.

The woodland collection from Big Sky Fiber Arts is a bulky carded Corriedale that works great for animals.

Locks and curls have a curly or wavy texture because they aren't carded. You can keep the natural color or dye them. This assortment is from Felting Farmer Lady. These can be applied to simulate wavy or curly animal coats, as well as manes and tails.

Locks or curls are wool that is cut from the sheep and left in its natural curly or wavy state.

Felting Surfaces

There are three options available when choosing surfaces on which to felt and work: foam, wool, or brush pads. If you're just starting out, the more common dense foam pads are a great choice. Once you begin creating more projects or if you'd like to have more flexibility with your needle felting, it's helpful to have all three options available.

Foam felting pads are the most common felting surfaces. These dense foam pads come in a variety of sizes and are a good choice for beginners. Many of these pads are made of petroleum-based polyurethane, but there are eco-friendly options such as Living Felt's Earth Harmony Series (which are soy-based). Eventually all foam pads will wear out and the little pieces of broken foam will stick to your felting projects, so they do need to be replaced occasionally.

Wool felting pads are 100 percent natural, are denser than foam, and last longer. Wool pads work very well with any needle felting project, although the process feels a bit different from felting on foam because the needles don't sink into the surface as much. You can also buy 100 percent wool "toppers" to cover your base wool felting pad and keep your

The three felting surfaces available are wool pads, dense foam pads (they are often made from polyurethane, but those shown here are eco-friendly foam), and felting brushes.

projects clean (for example, you'd use a white topper when working on a white project or a black topper when working on a dark project). I also like to use the toppers as a pad to straddle my animals on when working on the legs. I prefer using Living Felt's WOW (Wool on Wool) pads and WOWee wool toppers in brown, white, and black.

WOW pads come in a variety of sizes, with the larger sizes—up to 17" x 24" (43.2 x 61cm)—being ideal for wool paintings.

Felted Sky also offers a 100 percent wool felting mat that is 1½" (3.8cm) thick for the large size, 11" x 11" (28 x 28cm). It is so thick, you can actually felt on your lap without a hard surface. It also comes in a micro size and a mini size.

Brush felting pads are another type of felting surface. Felting on a brush is superior for felting flat items that require a lot of poking, such as cookie cutter figures or detailed ears, because the wool won't get stuck to the brush as it might on a dense surface. Brush felting pads also last for a very long time. You can find a variety of felting brushes with different materials like plastic or wood used as bases for the bristles.

Needles and Holders

Once you have fibers and a felting surface, you'll need at least one felting needle to create beautiful pieces of art and will also want to have a needle holder to make the process more comfortable and efficient.

Felting needles are straight needles without eyes that have notches or barbs on the pointed end that catch the scales on the wool, tangling and matting them together to turn the wool into felt. They are measured by gauge from coarse (32) to fine (42). The barbs on the needle can be arranged in three different patterns: star, spiral, or triangle. You can also purchase reverse needles with barbs pointed the opposite way to pull the fibers out and create a fuzzy effect. In general, coarser needles (36 or 38) are used to build up sculptural elements and finer needles (40 and 42) are used for the details, but which needles you use for which task is entirely up to you. A 38 spiral needle or 38 star needle is a good needle to begin with. My personal favorite is a 40 spiral needle and I use a 42 triangle needle for details. I also use reverse-felting needles to create texture and fur. Reverse-felting needles come in 36 or 38 gauge; I prefer 36. Needles can be color-coded by size or style and many suppliers

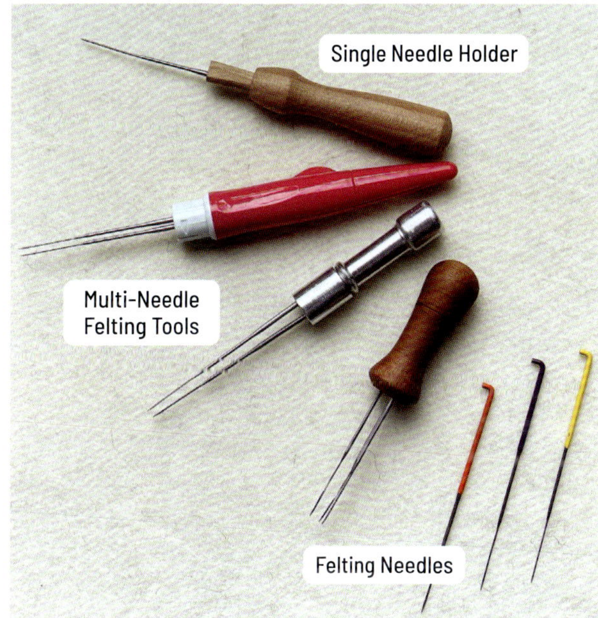

Needle holders are made to hold one or more needles. The needles themselves range from coarse to fine gauge (and some brands color their needles to indicate the gauge).

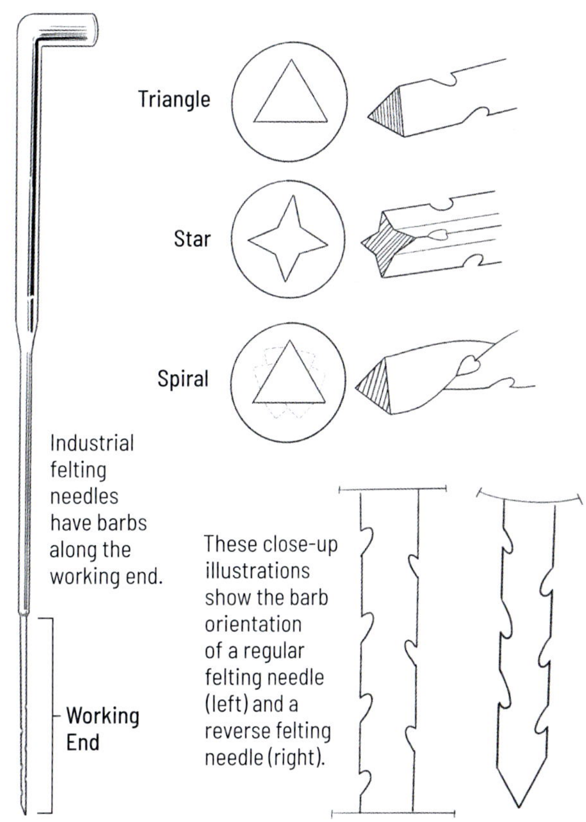

Felting needles are available in three shaft styles. The barbs run along the pointed edges of each shape.

offer sample packs, so you can experiment and learn what works best for you.

Needle holders are made of wood, metal, or plastic and are made to hold as few as one needle up to as many as five needles at once. Needle felting requires a lot of poking, so multi-needle tools are helpful. Different holders also space the needles differently, which will affect how they feel. I often work with two or three needles in my holder and use different holders for different needle gauges.

Other Supplies

Some of the projects require additional tools and supplies depending on whether you need to form a structural base or further shape the fibers. Some of these items are used to prepare the materials you will need for a project. For example, hand carders won't be listed in a project's supplies, but a blend of different wool colors will.

Toothpicks are useful temporary forms for creating larger spherical shapes. You can wrap the wool around them, then remove the toothpick and felt the piece.

Wire of different gauges and materials is used to create armatures (the base structures of three-dimensional sculptures). Wire can be made of aluminum, copper, or other metals and is sometimes coated in different colors. The gauge you use depends on the final piece. For instance, you may use thinner 24-gauge or 22-gauge wire for a bird's feet but use thicker 18-gauge wire to build the structure for a larger sculpture. I most often use 22-gauge or 20-gauge copper wire. You can find wire in craft stores and jewelry supply stores.

A sharp **wire cutter** is essential for cutting the correct lengths of wire you need for each piece.

Needle-nose pliers are useful for bending the wire into its initial shape and for making additional adjustments once it's covered in wool. In this book, I reference "flat-nosed" pliers to distinguish from round nose when flattening.

Small, sharp scissors like those used in sewing or embroidery are great for trimming hair and fur and cleaning up errant fibers. My favorite scissors for these tasks are the Karen Kay Buckley 4-inch Perfect Scissors I bought from Big Sky Fiber Arts.

Craft glue, basically any PVA (polyvinyl acetate) glue, is useful to dab on the end of your armature wire to hold the wool in place as you wrap it. You can also mix small amounts of glue with water to stiffen fibers, if needed.

A **50/ 50 hairspray and water mix** will also stiffen fibers and can be used to add texture to fur, wings, hair, or other elements.

An **awl** is great for making holes in felted wool pieces so you can more easily insert elements. For example, you'll use an awl to create a space to insert the pika's flower (see page 95).

A small set of **hand carders** will help you easily blend different colors of fiber to create your own unique shades and mixes.

A **hair straightening iron**, **mini iron**, **or iron** are used to flatten and smooth parts such as wings.

Alcohol markers with fine tips are useful for adding tiny details like whisker dots on a muzzle. They can be found at craft and art stores.

You can get **cookie cutters** in almost any shape you desire and they provide a nice, easy introduction to needle felting 2D items. In this book we use a howling wolf, bears, and trees.

While not essential to the basic process of needle felting, there are a number of other supplies that will improve your sculpting skills.

Techniques

Learning how to needle felt animals requires learning many techniques that create the various parts of the creature. Learning these individual techniques is the key to building your skill and many are transferable; for instance, the rounded ears of a bear are very similar to those of a mouse.

Practice these techniques before starting on your specific wildlife project. Before creating a needle felt animal, do your research. Study the animal from every angle in online images or in books. To enhance your creations further, take a trip to the zoo or to a national park for real-life wildlife viewing. As you build your skills, you may discover shortcuts or practices that work best for you. I am always working on improving my techniques.

Wrapping the Wire

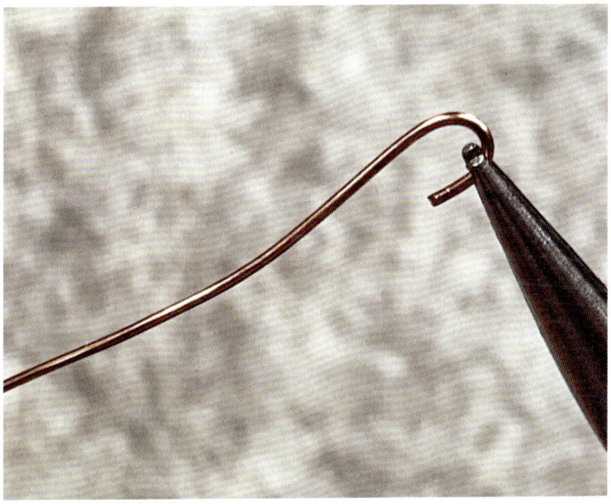

1. For most purposes—one exception is a bison horn—bend the end of a wire before wrapping, so it won't poke through the wool.

2. Glue the end and wrap around the bend. When wrapping wool, be certain to always wrap in the same direction, otherwise it will unravel.

Adding Bulk and Defining the Shape

1. Start shaping your figure by wrapping a layer around the wire, felting on both sides, and then wrapping another layer, felting on both sides. Add more layers, depending on the size of the figure.

2. To create body features such as a haunch or a hump, take a swatch of wool, roll it into a rounded shape and felt it lightly, then add to the figure and felt into place.

3. When making legs, wrap the wool and felt to a thickness slightly less than desired. For the final layer, to make the legs more realistic, lay the wool vertically down the leg and felt in place.

4. Felt the loose ends into the inside of the leg and felt in more fiber to cover the leg if needed.

Noses

1. Roll a small piece of wool into a ball with your fingers, then place the ball on the pad and felt and shape lightly with the needle. Inspect it to make sure it is the correct size.

2. When felting the nose onto the face, felt in around the edges first to retain the shape, and then felt in the rest of the nose to flatten it into place.

TIP

When felting in small details with strands of wool, place the strand, then poke in the area where you want the wool to go, and the wool will follow.

Mouths

1. There are many variations on animal mouths, but most mammals have a small line coming down from the nose, which is called a philtrum. Roll a thin strand of wool between your fingers and felt it into place under the nose.

2. Take a thin strand of wool and felt the center in place under the philtrum, then felt in the sides, whether upturned or downturned, to the length necessary. Cut the extra wool off. With felted animals, usually smaller mouths look better.

Eyes

1. To create a basic eye, roll a loose ball of wool, place on the face, and felt around the edges first to create the eye shape. Once you're satisfied with the shape, felt the rest of the eye into place.

2. To further enhance the eye shape, roll a thin strand of wool between your fingers and place it above the eye and felt in. You can also do this at the bottom of the eye. You may felt the strand a little longer at the eye corners for a tapered eye.

3. To create the lights in the eyes, take a small piece of white wool and roll it between your fingers. If you have trouble getting it tiny enough, cut the ball in half and roll again. Felt the eye light into the top center of the eye.

Making and Attaching Ears

1. Most animals' ears are round or triangular, or somewhere in between. To create pointed ears, fold a piece of wool and pinch the top, then poke the shape on both sides, adding more wool to the center if the ear is too thin. With rounded ears, start the shape by rolling the wool into a soft U.

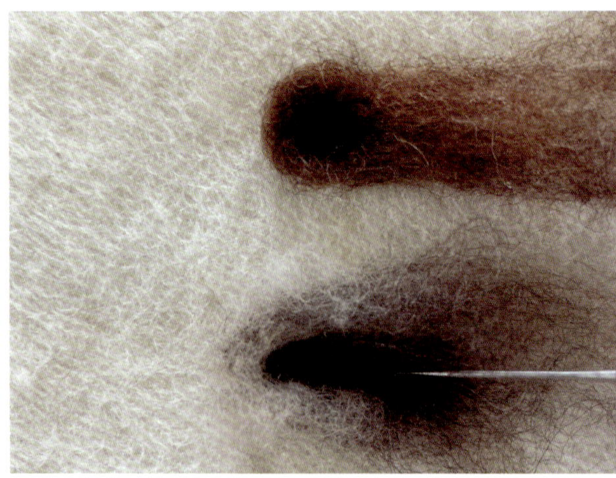

2. Felt in a darker wool, or sometimes a pink wool, to the middle, following the shape of the ear. For some animals, you will add a layer of white wool prior to the dark or pink center.

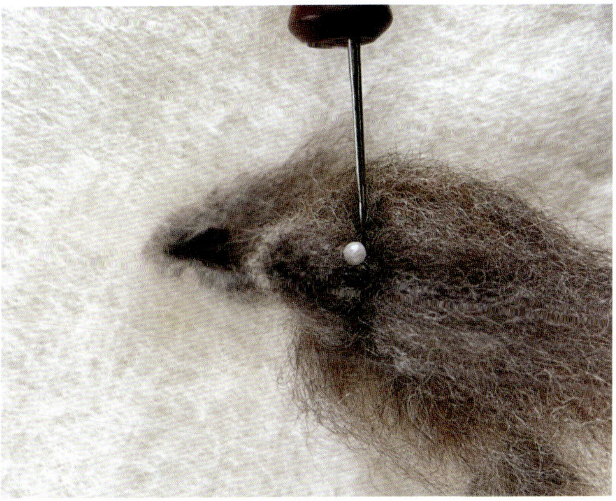

3. When placing the ear, it helps to use a ball-head pin to anchor it before felting. Most animal ears are angled a bit with the outside edge slightly further from the nose. Felt the excess wool into the back of the head, close to the bottom of the ear.

4. Felt the front of the ear into the head by first felting vigorously in the middle of the ear, and then more lightly along the edges. If the ears are too big, you can either felt more in the back, pushing the ear down further into the head, or cut them carefully with scissors.

Adding Fluff or Fur

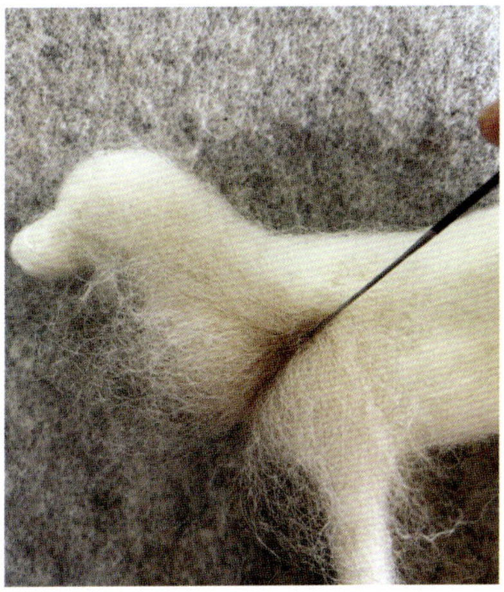

1. Layering long fibers, such as merino or alpaca top, creates a furry look, either over the whole body or just under the neck. To do this, take a thin swatch of fiber, place it, and felt a line back and forth along the center until it is fully attached.

2. Fold the layer over the line and lightly felt along the top.

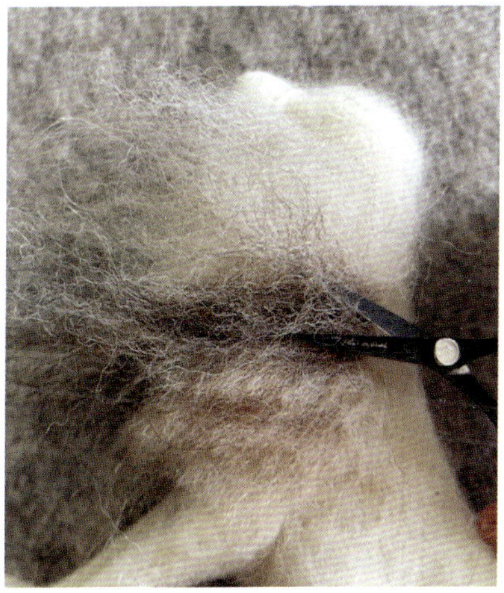

3. Add more layers in the same manner, and then trim with scissors. For most animals in this book, one or two layers will do.

4. Another method to create fur or fuzziness is using reverse-felting needles. Take a 36-gauge reverse needle (you can also use two in a multi-needle holder) and poke repeatedly up and down and across in the area you want fuzzy. Then trim the fur with scissors.

5. For a softer look, angle your reverse-felting needle so you are "combing" the fibers and gently pulling them. Then trim.

Smoothing and Texturizing

1. To prevent visible holes in your animal, use a fine-gauged needle such as a 40 to apply the top coat.

2. One way to smooth your creation is to use a mini iron, but please be careful; they are very hot.

3. A mixture of hairspray and water can both smooth and texture your sculpture. To smooth, spray lightly on the figure, then use your fingers to smooth the fibers in place.

4. To texture fur, spray lightly and use your needle or multi-needle tool to puff out and arrange the fur. Trim any fibers that stretched after combing.

Dyeing Wool

You can purchase dyed wool in a rainbow of colors, but sometimes you want a particular fiber in a particular color—dyeing wool yourself is the answer. Dyeing wool and other natural fibers is fun but it can be challenging. The chemistry doesn't always work how you envision, and different fibers pick up varying tones from the dye. Locks and curls don't dye evenly—they pick up more dye at the ends than at the roots. Mixing different dye colors can be tricky as the fiber may pick up more of one color than the other. With all that being said, it is fun to play with dyeing wool and definitely worth the experimentation.

The easiest method for dyeing wool is to use acid dyes. There are many different brands available from suppliers. Each brand includes directions on the package but be aware that these directions are usually for larger amounts of wool than you would be using for needle felting. You will need to reduce the amount of water and dye used based on how much fiber you are actually dyeing. Mini measuring spoon sets (which range from ¼ teaspoon down to 1/64 teaspoon) are quite useful for measuring dyeing ingredients. Some dye brands also provide dye mixing charts, but you will still need to reduce the ingredient amounts. You can also just play with different ratios of dye to water and learn by doing.

SUPPLIES

- Stovetop
- Cooking pots
- Wool
- Acid dye
- Vinegar or citric acid
- Gloves
- Bowls
- Tongs
- Mini measuring spoon set

NOTE

Do not use your regular cooking implements for dyeing fiber. Have a special set of cooking pots, bowls, tongs, and measuring spoons that you use solely for dyeing.

Hang dyed wool up to dry. Machine drying would felt the wool.

Start with the package directions, adjusting the amounts as needed. The directions will generally involve the following process:

1. Soak the wool in a bowl of lukewarm water.
2. Heat water in pot to just below boiling.
3. Add the dye and stir.
4. Add the wool and stir gently. Do not overagitate since that would felt the wool.
5. Stir in the vinegar or citric acid.
6. Watch and gently stir the wool until it's reached the desired color.
7. Remove the wool with tongs, rinse it, squeeze out the water, then hang it to dry.

TIP

You can blend multiple different fibers using hand carders but be careful not to overload them.

Blending Wool

Blending wool is another way to create custom wool colors. For instance, blending a brown fiber with a copper fiber could result in the perfect color you need to create a red fox. Blending different fibers to achieve unique textures and colors can also create a more natural look for animal fur or hair. You can blend wool by hand with no tools or by using hand carders. Hand carders are more efficient and create a more thorough blend.

To blend by hand without tools, simply lay a length of one fiber on top of another, then gently pull at both ends. Repeat until you achieve the desired effect.

To blend using hand carders, lay a thin layer of one fiber on one of the carders, then lay a thin layer of the other fiber on top. Use the second carder to comb the wool by lifting out and up. Continue to comb until all the fiber is on the second carder, then remove the wool.

Projects

These projects progress in difficulty to help you build your skills. First, you'll start by using cookie cutters as templates to create simple two-dimensional felted shapes, then you'll begin to create three-dimensional pieces using small, straight wires and rolling techniques. The next set of projects uses more complicated detailing techniques. The later projects are more structurally intricate and include a lot more fine details and realistic elements.

BLACK BEAR AND PINE MOBILE

DIFFICULTY: Beginner

The black bear is the most common bear species in North America and is often the one you're most likely to encounter in your own backyard. Their shy nature and adaptability give them an endearing quality, even as they roam vast landscapes. Black bears inhabit a wide range, from the misty forests of the Pacific Northwest to the rugged Appalachian Mountains, stretching as far south as Florida and Texas. Historically, their range covered nearly all of North America. Today, they thrive in many national parks, where their lives intertwine with iconic ecosystems. In Yosemite Valley, generations of black bears have grown bold around campers, while in Great Smoky Mountains National Park, they climb towering pine trees for safety and forage among dense understories. Pine forests are critical to their survival, offering shelter, seasonal food sources like nuts and berries, and safe spots for hibernation. In Glacier Bay National Park, black bears use their strong claws to dig for roots and insects beneath forest floors, demonstrating their remarkable adaptability. These parks not only protect black bears but also preserve the pine-dominated habitats that sustain them.

Using cookie cutters to create felted shapes is an easy beginner project. Felting into a mold can get you familiar with the process of poking and firming wool into felt. While this project arranges the bears and trees into a mobile, you can also hang them individually as ornaments, and they make very special little gifts for nature lovers.

SUPPLIES

- Foam or brush pad
- Bear and pine tree cookie cutters
- Felting needles, 38 star or 40 spiral
- Multi-needle felting tool (optional)
- Scissors
- Green wool locks
- Carded roving in the following colors:
  - Various shades of green
  - Dark brown
  - Tan
  - Black
  - White

Pine Trees

1. Place your pine tree cookie cutter on a pad, or preferably a brush, and fill with green wool. Felt in place vigorously, being certain to felt into the edges.

2. Felt a thick layer of brown wool into the trunk of the tree. Be certain to poke enough to create a solid trunk. Don't felt too much brown into the green branches as it will poke through.

3. Felt in another thick layer of green wool over the tree trunk.

4. Gently remove the cookie cutter and the tree and turn over. Fluff out the branches by combing with the felting needle.

5. Take your green wool locks and gently separate them; lay them down on the tree in a sweeping angle and felt in place.

6. If you are not using locks for texture, you can blend two shades of green together. See Blending Wool on page 18.

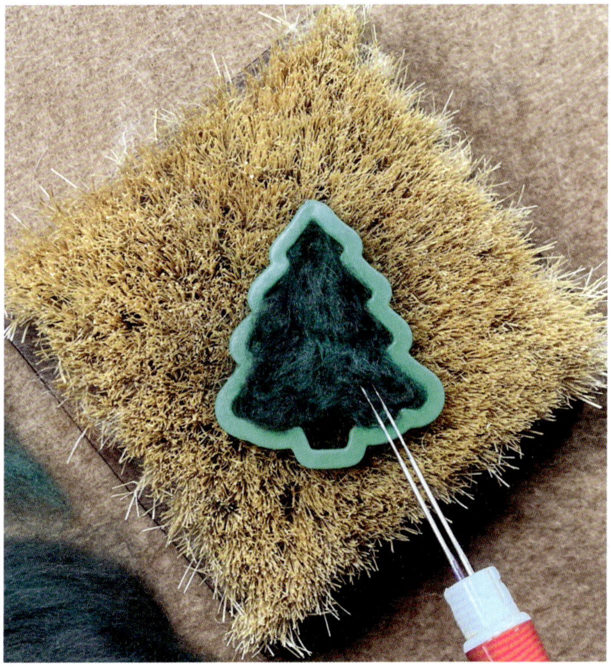

7. Felt the two-tone green into the tree and the trunk as shown previously.

8. Flip over and trim the edges of the tree with scissors.

Black Bears

1. Lay your bear cookie cutter on a pad, fill with brown wool, and start poking with your needle, being sure to felt vigorously, especially around the edges. When working with cookie cutters, hold them in place with the hand that is not felting.

2. Felt in two to three layers until your bear is nice and thick.

3. Turn the bear over and adjust any areas that have lost shape. For instance, the feet may need to be bent a little and felted around the edges. The ear may need more felting, or you can create a new ear (see Making and Attaching Ears, page 14). The edges may also need to be defined by felting along the edges.

4. Place a small swatch of tan wool on the muzzle and felt in place, folding the loose ends over the back of muzzle and felting in.

5. Roll a small ball of black wool and felt into the tip of the muzzle (see Noses, page 13).

6. Roll another small ball of black and felt into the face right above the muzzle for an eye. Add eye lights as described on page 14.

7. Take a wisp of white wool and felt into the neck in a V shape for a chevron.

8. Fold and felt a small piece of brown wool, and then felt into place for a tail.

9. Assemble your trees and bears, attach a string with a sewing needle (I used green thread), and hang them from a branch. Your mobile is complete!

WILDLIFE FINGER PUPPETS

DIFFICULTY: Beginner

Wildlife finger puppets can spark hours of imaginative storytelling for young adventurers. Picture yourself in a national park, gathered around a campfire, each person holding a puppet that represents an animal found in these wild places. A gray wolf puppet might inspire tales of Yellowstone, where wolves roam the valleys and play a vital role in balancing ecosystems. An arctic hare puppet could bring to life the snowy landscapes of Denali or Rocky Mountain National Park, where hares dart through pine forests and change their coats with the seasons. And the polar bear cub puppet is a perfect way to imagine the icy wilderness of Alaska's Arctic national parks, where polar bears depend on sea ice and frigid waters for survival.

Finger puppets are a beginner project. The first few steps are the same for all animals in this lesson. Be sure to read the sections on ears, eyes, nose, mouth and fluff in the Techniques chapter (starting on page 11). You can also expand the options with some adjustments and make the wolf into a fox or coyote; the hare can be a cottontail bunny and the polar bear cub can become a black bear or grizzly bear. Stuff a little wool into the puppet, and it is free standing.

SUPPLIES

- Felting pad
- Felting needles
- Multi-needle felting tool
- Scissors
- Core wool
- Carded roving in the following colors:
  - White
  - Gray
  - Black
  - Taupe
  - Brown
  - Fawn or light brown
  - Dark brown
  - Dark gray
- One 3" x ¾" x ¾" (7.6 x 1.9 x 1.9cm) piece of foam
- One 2½" x 3½" (6.4 x 8.9cm) rectangle white 100% wool fabric per puppet

Foam Bases

1. A little foam base can be cut from an old piece of felting foam or from a sponge. Start by wrapping the piece of wool around the foam and leaving about 1" (2.5cm) extending above the foam.

2. Wrap a strand of wool fairly tight around the top of the foam to create a neck. Roll a piece of wool around the head and felt in.

3. Wrap wool around the entire body and felt in.

Arctic Hare

1. Wrap a piece of wool from front to back to start shaping the head and felt in.

2. Roll two little rounds of wool and felt into the sides of the face, just under where the eyes will go.

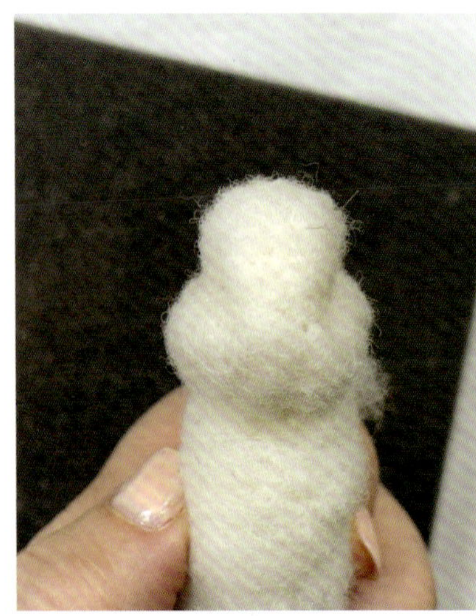

3. Felt in a piece of wool across the cheeks and nose to smooth the face.

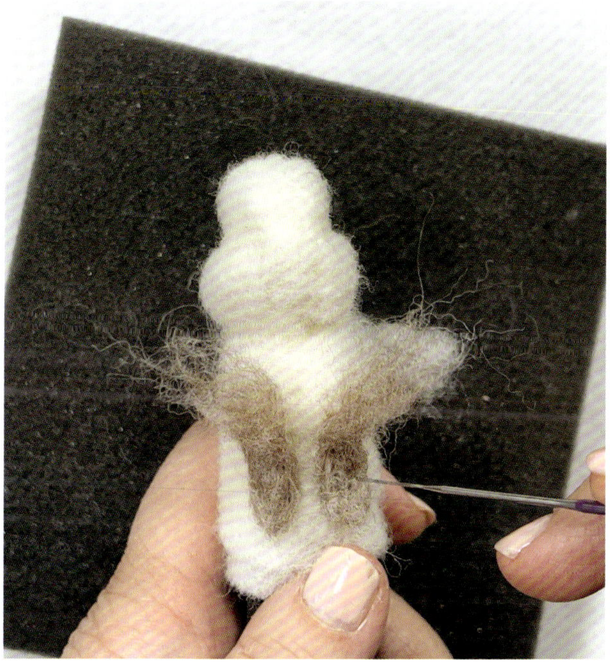

4. Fold two small lengths of taupe wool and felt into the front for the legs.

5. Fold two longer pieces of brown wool and felt on both sides for the ears and felt white wool into the center (see page 14).

6. Felt the ears into the back of the head and cut off excess wool so only the ears are brown.

7. Form a soft triangular nose of taupe wool and felt into the face.

8. Outline the nose by felting in a strand of dark brown wool. Then take a strand of dark brown, felt a line under the nose, and separate the strand into a mouth and felt in. Cut off excess.

9. Roll a black piece of wool and place in the center of the face above the cheek. Felt into a tapered shape. Add tiny white lights to the eyes (see page 14). Then felt a piece of wool loosely under the neck for fluff.

10. Add a swatch of wool vertically in the back and along the sides to round out the hare.

11. Fold a small piece of wool, felt it, and attach it to the bottom of the hare for a tail.

Polar Bear Cub

1. After creating the foam base (see page 28), roll a ½" (1.2cm) piece of wool to create a muzzle and felt on each side, keeping it rounded.

2. Felt the piece firmly from the top of the muzzle where the nose will be, leaving the bottom looser.

3. Felt the muzzle into the bottom of the head by felting around the perimeter of the muzzle and attaching securely.

4. Take a piece of wool and felt from under the muzzle and across the top of the head.

5. Create a round head by felting more layers of wool across the top.

6. Felt in layers of wool from the muzzle to the back of the head.

7. Fold two lengths of wool for the legs and felt, adding extra rounds of wool at the paws. Attach and felt into the body at an angle.

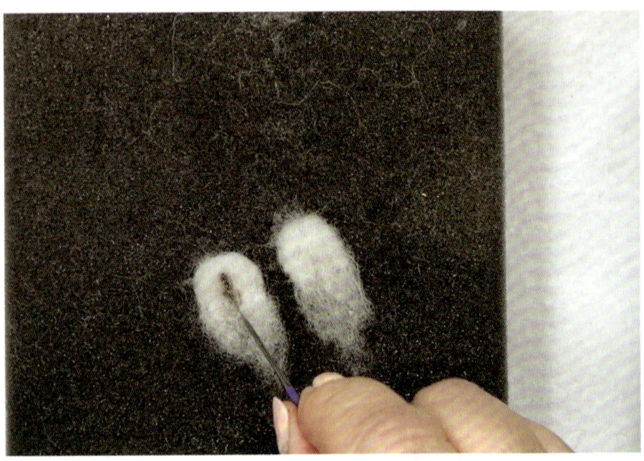

8. Felt two small rounds of wool and add a small piece of gray to the middle for ears (see page 14).

9. Felt in the ears to the far sides of the head. Roll a small ball of black wool and felt in place for a nose. Take a strand of gray and felt under the nose into a slight smile.

10. Felt a small swatch of gray wool above the nose. Roll two small round black balls and felt in for eyes, just above the muzzle. Add eye lights.

11. Felt in some fluff to the front and back of the cub. Then felt a small swatch of wool into the cub for a tiny tail.

Gray Wolf

1. Start with the foam base and roll two legs with white wool and felt.

2. Felt the legs into the body.

3. Create a muzzle like the polar bear cub, but this should be longer. Felt the muzzle into the head and add a piece of wool across the nose and into the side of the head. Poke repeatedly around the muzzle to firm and slim.

4. Fold a piece of wool and felt in along the top on each side of the face to fill out.

5. Felt a piece of wool across the face to blend in.

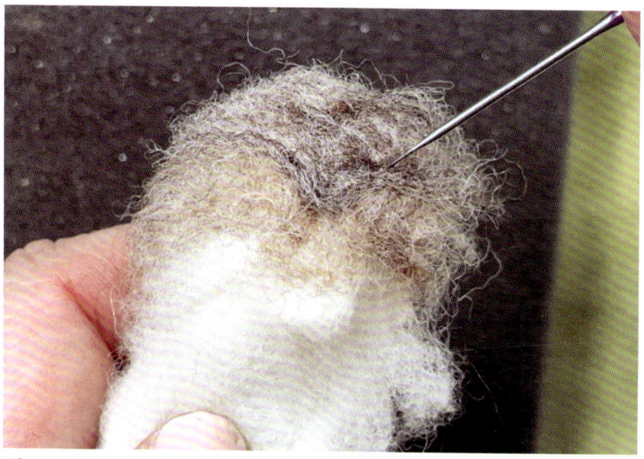

6. Felt in some lighter brown wool down the nose and across the middle of the face. Then felt in gray wool above the lighter color, creating slight arches above where the eyes will be.

7. Form two triangles of gray wool, felt, and then add triangles of white wool, felt in, and finish with triangles of darker grey wool. Attach the ears to the top of the head and trim if needed.

8. Roll a piece of black wool for a nose, felt in place, and use a strip of dark gray to create an upturned mouth. Create indentations that slightly angle up towards the ears with your needle to place the eyes.

9. Create two small rounds of black for eyes, Use your needle to poke and angle the eyes slightly upward and add lights.

10. Felt in gray wool along the top of the leg and angle out to the back. Felt in gray rounds for the haunches.

11. Add a layer of wool under the neck for fluff (see Adding Fluff or Fur on page 15) and trim in a V shape. Felt in two rounds of white wool for the paws—remember that wolves have large paws.

12. Create a tail by taking a swatch of black wool, adding gray above it, wrapping into a round, and felting on all sides. Then remove the wolf from the foam and felt the tail into the inside and back.

13. Your puppets are ready to wear!

HOWLING WOLF STARRY NIGHT WOOL PAINTING

DIFFICULTY: Beginner

This wool painting draws inspiration from the breathtaking landscapes of America's national parks, paired with a starry night theme that evokes the mystery of the wild. Wolves, often seen as symbols of wilderness, roam some of the most iconic parks in the country. I once visited Voyageurs National Park hoping to hear the haunting call of a wolf—a sound that defines the untamed spirit of the Northwoods. While I didn't hear one that night, I found wonder at the International Wolf Center in Ely, Minnesota, where visitors can learn about these elusive creatures. Wolves also thrive in Yellowstone, Grand Teton, Denali, and Glacier National Parks, where they play a vital role in maintaining healthy ecosystems. The gray wolf's story is one of resilience: nearly eradicated from the lower 48 states due to persecution and habitat loss, they now occupy only about 10% of their historic range. Thanks to protections under the Endangered Species Act and reintroduction efforts, wolves have made a comeback—but they still face challenges and remain a powerful reminder of the delicate balance between humans and nature.

This wool painting is easier than it looks. The next few pages will introduce you to applying wool in layers to create a painting effect. It is a great starter to wool painting, and you can make it your own by adjusting the color scheme.

SUPPLIES

- Large felting pad or foam 11" x 14" (28 x 35.6cm) or larger
- Felting needles
- Multi-needle felting tool
- Scissors
- Blue (or white) piece of felt cut into 11" x 14" (28 x 35.6cm)
- Wolf cookie cutter, 3.5" to 4" (8.9 to 10.2cm)
- Carded roving in the following colors:
  - Green or variegated green
  - Variegated gray
  - Gray-brown
  - Black
- Top wool in the following colors:
  - Dark blue
  - Medium blue
  - Bright blue
  - Light blue
  - Light yellow
  - Bright yellow
  - Brown
- White core wool
- Piece of heavy frame glass from 11" x 14" (28 x 35.6cm) or larger (optional)
- Iron (optional)
- Drinking glass or round cookie cutters, 2¼" (5.7cm) and 3" (7.6cm) diameter

TIP

If you dye your own wool (see page 17), the hot bath from dyeing will make the wool easier to spread in thin layers across the felt. If you buy pre-dyed wool, you can put it in a hot pot of water for a few minutes, dry it, and it will spread nicely.

1. Start with the blue felt that you can purchase or dye yourself. If you dye it, cut the wool at least 2" (5.1cm) larger as it will shrink when dyed. You can start with white felt, but it will require more layers of blue to cover.

2. Take 12" (30.5cm) lengths of bright blue wool, spread them into a thin layer, and lay them horizontally across the felt.

3. Felt along each edge of the painting. Felt lightly across the painting so as not to create too many needle holes.

4. One method to flatten the wool is to lay a glass frame on top and rub your hands back and forth over it. You can also keep the glass on the wool overnight, weighted with a heavy book.

5. Another method for flattening the wool and eliminating the needle holes is to iron carefully on the wool setting.

6. Start creating the mountains toward the bottom third of the painting by laying a length of medium blue in a peaked shape and felt in along the edges.

7. Shape a loose triangular peak with light blue and felt in place.

8. Sweep across another medium blue peak and felt along the edges.

9. Take some light blue wisps and lay across the mountains for texture; felt lightly.

10. Add a swatch of green under the mountains, then felt along the edges and lightly in the middle.

11. Create the rocks by laying three lengths of gray in a curved manner and felting in place.

12. Lay a thick length of brown wool vertically along the outer edge for a tree, but don't felt in yet. Position your wolf cookie cutter to see what looks best.

13. Place the 2¼" (5.7cm) glass in the top right corner and trace a circle around the rim with the felting needle.

14. Felt in the light yellow wool inside the circle.

15. Add some bright yellow wool to the center.

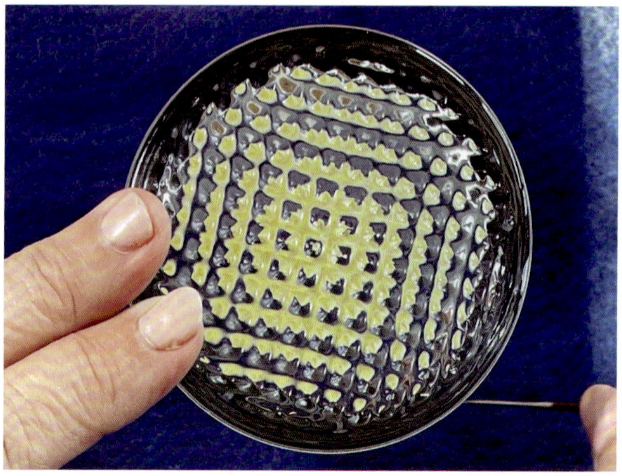

16. Trace an outline over the moon with the larger glass.

17. Felt in wisps of yellow wool along the circle, and then felt in more circles and wisps around the moon.

18. Felt in some dark blue wisps across the sky. Use your imagination!

19. Felt in small, loose circles of light yellow across the sky and add a wisp of light blue above the mountains.

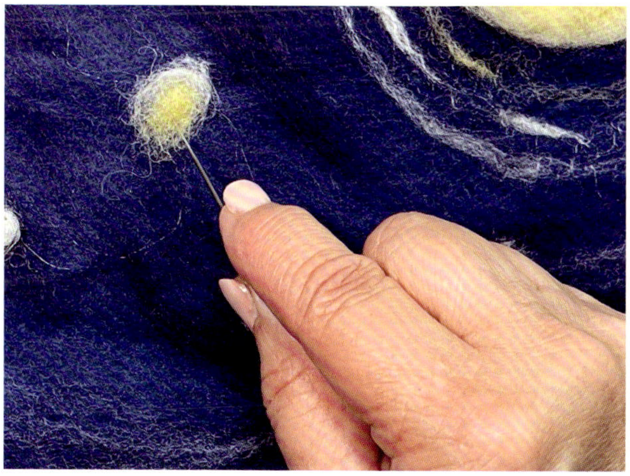

20. Felt in some bright yellow to the center of the stars.

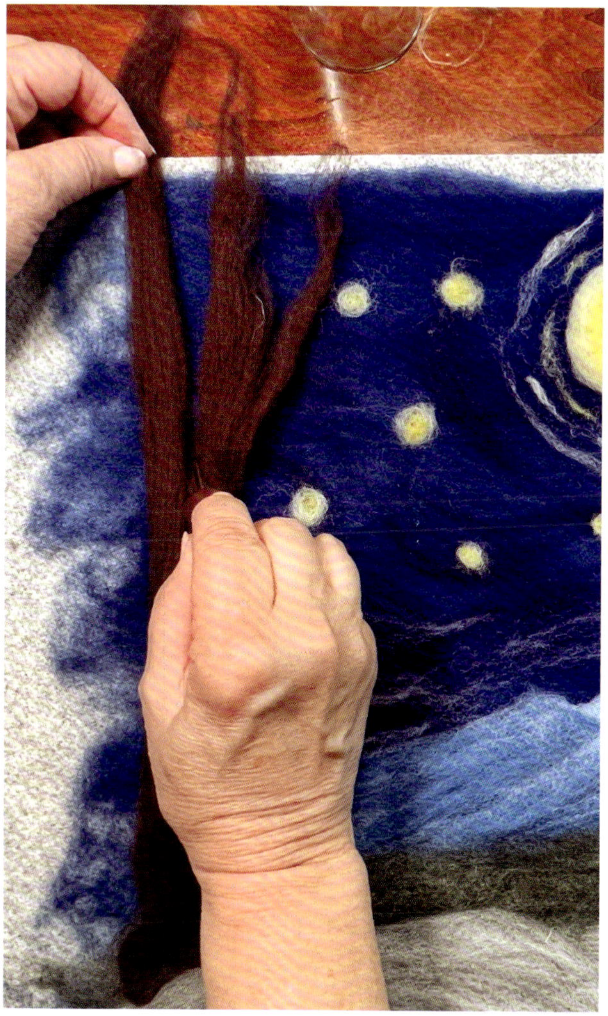

21. Felt the edges of the tree all the way to the top on the left and about two-thirds up on the right. Separate the right limb of the tree and break it into two limbs.

22. Pull a piece from the edge and twist, lay down, and felt in place. Repeat with another branch.

23. Felt some lines into the tree for bark. You do not need to add extra wool; the felting will create lines. Then once the tree is placed, add more tiny stars.

24. Place the wolf and felt all along the inside so you have an outline and a flat surface for the wool layers.

25. Start filling in the wolf with white wool. Felt very thin pieces along the legs, mouth, and ear so they don't get too thick. Remove the cookie cutter. Felt along the edges to shape the wolf where necessary. **Note**: This cookie cutter only showed three legs, so I felted in another back leg.

26. Felt a little gray wool to the center of the ear.

27. Add thin wisps of gray-brown as shown across the top of the head, chest, and streaks across the chest. Add gray to the back end. Add black loosely at the tail tip and gray loosely above.

28. Felt in a small black nose and a thin layer of black along the inside edge of the mouth. Felt in a small black strand to create an arched, closed eye.

29. Turn the painting over and felt in the loose wool to the back. Wool paintings look good in a shadow box frame without glass, but you can also place them behind glass, which will create a more flattened-looking painting.

ARCTIC SEAL PUP

DIFFICULTY: Beginner–Intermediate

Most seal pups are born with a soft white coat, and this wool creation is inspired by the ringed seal—a species that inhabits the icy waters of the Bering and Chukchi Seas in Alaska. These seals depend on sea ice for resting and protection, making them a vital part of the Arctic ecosystem. Sadly, ringed seals are listed as threatened due to melting sea ice and reduced snowfall. They share their frigid habitat with other species like ribbon seals, which roam the open Bering Sea, and harp seals, found in the North Atlantic. While ringed seals are elusive and live in some of the most remote wilderness areas, you can imagine their world in places like Alaska's Arctic national parks, including Gates of the Arctic and Kobuk Valley, where vast frozen landscapes provide critical habitat for Arctic wildlife. Though you may never encounter a seal pup outside of a zoo or research station, creating your own miniature is a way to celebrate these resilient creatures and the pristine parks that protect their fragile environment.

This mini seal pup is a beginner–intermediate project in which you will learn how to shape a marine animal, create flippers, and add whiskers.

SUPPLIES

- Felting pad
- Felting needles
- Multi-needle felting tool
- Awl or scissors
- White core wool or white carded roving
- Carded wool roving in the following colors:
  - Medium gray
  - Gray
  - Black
- Black horsehair
- 20-gauge copper wire
- Craft glue
- Flat-nosed pliers
- Arctic Seal Pup template (page 115)

1. Cut a 5" (12.7cm) piece of 20-gauge wire. As in Wrapping the Wire on page 11, bend both ends, dab with glue, and roll a length of wool from top to bottom. Felt in place.

2. Roll more wool in the center to begin to round the body and felt in place.

3. Bend into a seal shape as pictured. Then use an awl or scissors to make a hole behind the chest.

4. Insert a 5.5" (14cm) length of 20-gauge wire through the chest.

5. Wrap more wool around the chest and middle and felt to make it rounded and solid.

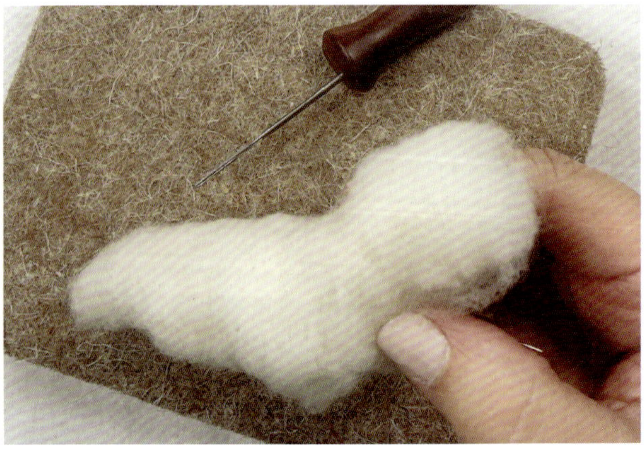

6. Start to create a rounded head by wrapping wool around the head and felting in place.

7. Roll a small piece of wool and felt it.

8. Felt the ball into the head for a small muzzle. Add a swatch of wool over the head and muzzle to the chest and felt in place. Felt around the muzzle to define it.

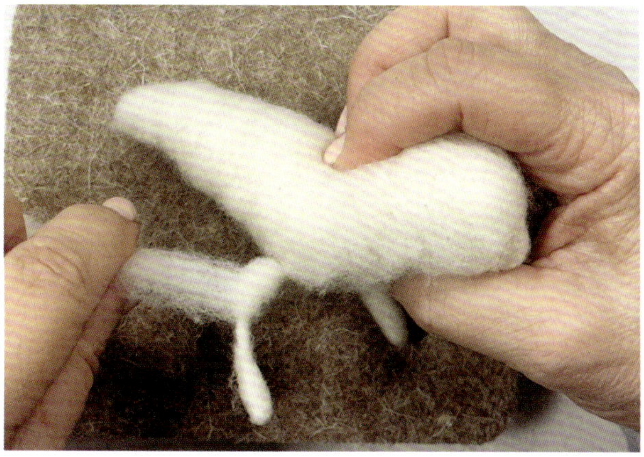

9. After bending back the ends of the flippers and gluing, roll wool around them and felt in.

10. Place a swatch of folded wool over the flipper and felt in place to create a squared flipper.

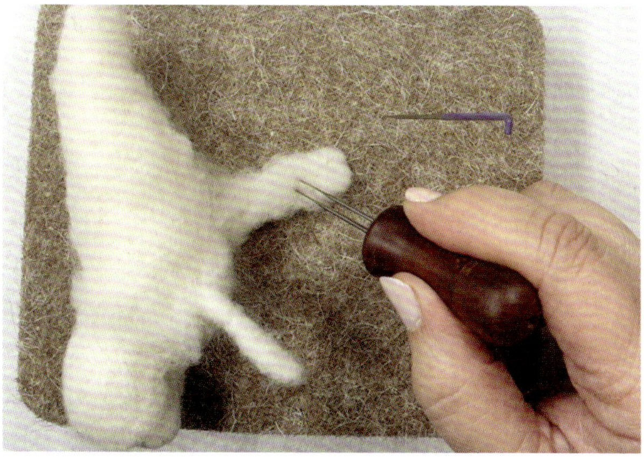

11. Fold excess wool over the flipper and felt in the back side. Repeat with the other flipper.

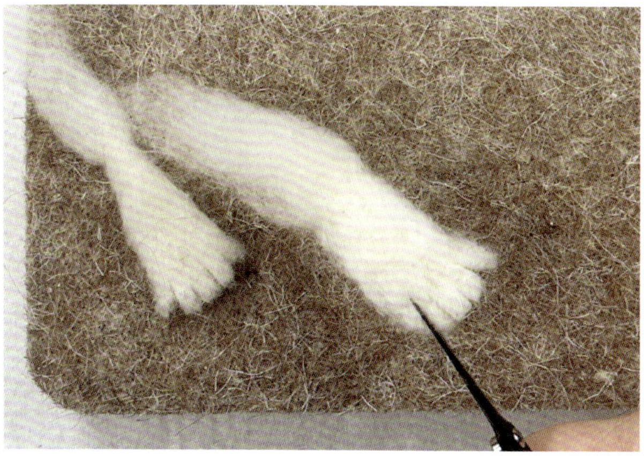

12. For the back flippers, take two swatches of wool, fold them over, and felt the bottom 1.5" (3.8cm) very vigorously on both sides to create a flat, solid felt. Then cut four shallow slices into the ends to create toes.

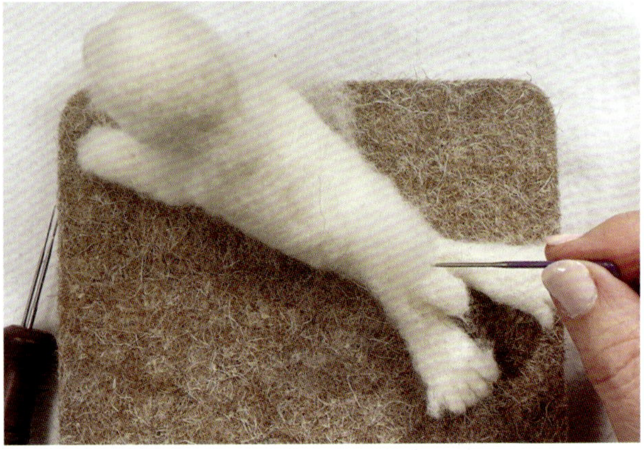

13. Attach the back flippers by felting into place. Then felt a small piece of wool for a tail and attach.

14. Add more wool on top of the back from chest to tail and felt in.

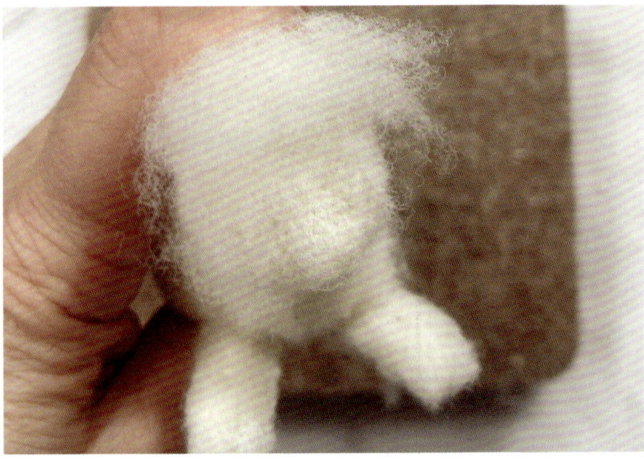

15. Add swatches of wool from the front to the back of the head and along the cheeks and felt in, keeping a rounded shape for the head.

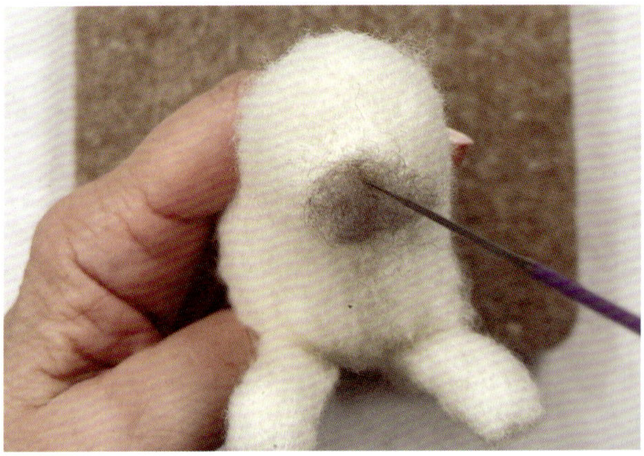

16. Form an oval piece of medium gray wool and felt into a muzzle.

17. Roll a small piece of gray wool into a nose and felt at the top of the muzzle.

18. Outline the nose shape with a thin piece of black wool and felt in place. Then place a thin piece of black wool in a curved shape under the nose and felt in place. Cut off excess.

19. Felt in a tiny piece of gray wool above the nose.

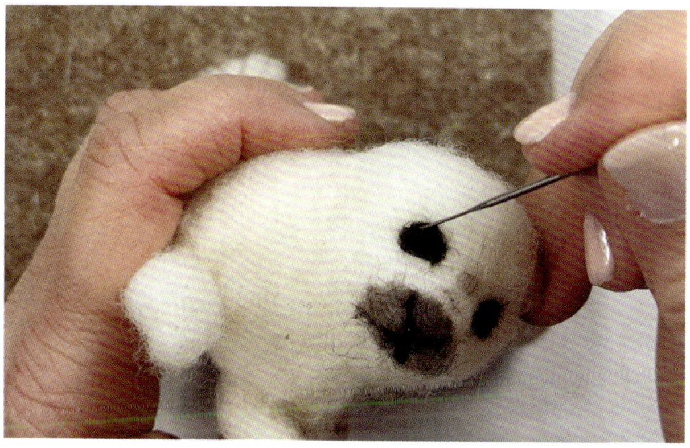

20. Roll two small balls of black wool and position in place for the eyes. Felt the eyes into place and poke downward along the outer corner to create a more realistic eye.

21. Add tiny white lights to eyes as explained on page 14. Felt in two tiny swatches of gray wool above the eyes and cut off excess.

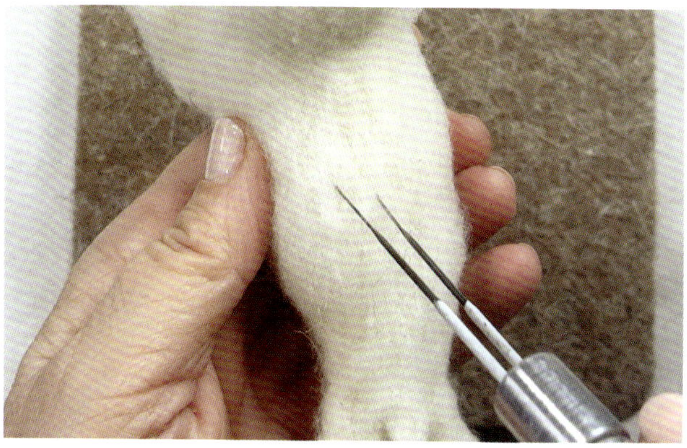

22. Gently pull out a bit of fuzz all over with reverse needles as explained on page 16.

23. Thread a needle with a piece of black horsehair and make a knot about 2" (5.1cm) from the end. Thread the horsehair through the muzzle, and it will be caught by the knot. Do three or more sets of whiskers and trim them.

24. Felt in four thin lines on the front of the flippers to create toes. Now the baby seal is all done!

NAPPING BISON

DIFFICULTY: Beginner–Intermediate

The bison stands as a powerful symbol of strength, resilience, and abundance. Revered as a sacred animal by many Native American cultures, it embodies generosity and harmony with nature. Once driven to the brink of extinction by European settlers, the bison has made a remarkable recovery and now thrives in the protected landscapes of our national parks as a living reminder of conservation and renewal. Yellowstone National Park is home to the largest herd in the United States, about 5,000 animals, where bison have roamed continuously since prehistoric times. Visitors to Yellowstone or Grand Teton National Park can often see these majestic creatures grazing in open valleys or crossing rivers, a sight that connects us to the wild heritage of North America. Other parks, such as Badlands and Wind Cave, also safeguard bison herds, ensuring their survival for future generations. These parks not only protect bison but also preserve the grassland ecosystems that sustain them. (And remember to admire from a distance; never approach or try to pet them!)

This Napping Bison is a beginner–intermediate project. It introduces needle felters to creating an animal in a lying-down pose, building the body structure, and making the horns.

SUPPLIES

- Felting pad
- Felting needles
- Multi-needle felting tool
- Scissors
- Core wool
- Carded roving in the following colors:
  - Dark brown
  - Medium brown
  - Light reddish brown
  - Light gray
  - Medium gray
  - Black
- Black or dark brown long fiber top wool, i.e., merino or alpaca
- 20-gauge copper wire
- Craft glue
- Hairspray/water mix
- Flat-nosed pliers
- Napping Bison template (page 115)

Horns

1. Cut a 2¼" (5.7cm) length of wire, coat with glue, and wrap from end to end with light gray wool.

2. Add extra glue along the bottom of each horn and wrap another layer to thicken the horns.

3. You can add a little extra glue at the tips and roll with your fingers to taper. Set the horn aside to dry.

Bison

1. Cut a 12½" (31.8cm) piece of wire, glue the ends, and wrap with one coat of core wool. Bend the wire into the shape pictured. You can refer to the template on page 115.

2. Wrap core wool around the entire body and head and felt in place.

3. Insert a 5½" (14cm) piece of wire through the back of the body for the back legs.

4. Start wrapping the body with medium brown wool and felt in. (With dark animals, using dark wool for the core prevents white bits from poking out.)

5. Start building the head by wrapping wool across the nose from front to back, and then across the nose from the neck to the top of the head.

6. Fold a swatch of wool and felt along the sides of the face on both sides to create bulk.

7. Make the head larger in the back by felting in a swatch across the top back of the head.

8. Roll a length of wool on the back legs back and forth until the leg is adequately thick, then felt into place.

9. Wrap a very small piece of light gray wool at the end of both back feet for hooves and felt.

10. Create the front folded legs by folding over a thick swatch of wool, felting it on all sides, then rolling another swatch along the bottom inch for more thickness and felting until firm.

11. After both legs are done, felt the loose fiber into the side of the bison and vigorously felt the bottom of the legs into the body. Felt the bottom of the legs so they lie flat.

12. Roll and felt in a round of wool at the top of the hump to make it more prominent.

13. Felt in a swatch of wool from the legs and over the hump to add thickness.

14. Felt in a thick swatch of wool along the bottom of the bison.

15. Create a round for the hip and felt it on the pad, then felt it into the bison.

16. Felt in dark brown wool over front folded leg, along the bottom of the stomach, and over the hip.

17. Felt light reddish brown wool over the hump and along the back, then felt small wisps of medium brown wool between the dark and light to blend in.

18. Place the horns toward the back of the head, then take a long swatch of wool to wrap around them, crisscrossing, and felt in place.

19. Place a swatch of wool over the head and felt in. Felt more wool along the sides of the face to blend in texture.

20. Create an oval round of the medium gray and felt into place for the nose.

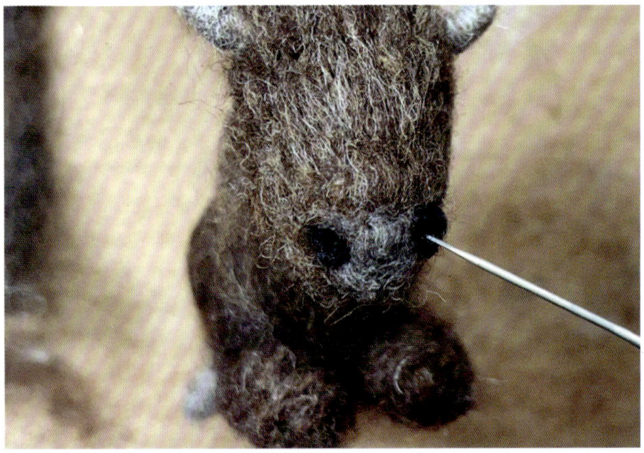

21. Felt in two elongated black ovals along the edges for nostrils.

22. Felt in a strand of black wool under the nostrils for a mouth.

23. Take a length of dark brown wool and felt in place from the nose to the top of the head.

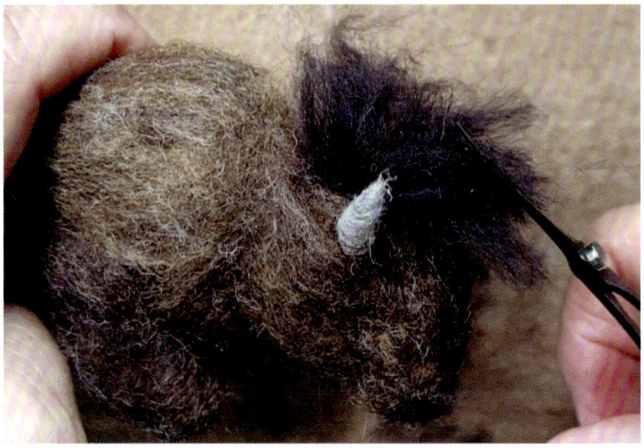

24. Add two or three layers of dark brown top wool for fluff at top of head (see page 15). Then trim the hair on top of the head.

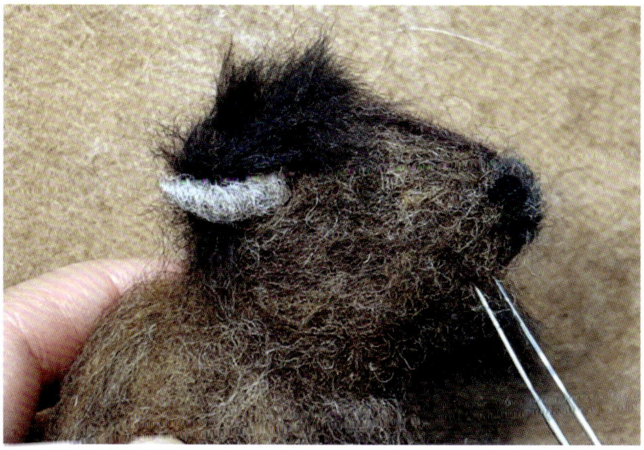

25. Add one layer of fluff under the chin and trim it. Comb a little of the brown wool with your needle over the beard to blend it in.

26. Felt in a small oval of light brown near the horn for an eye patch.

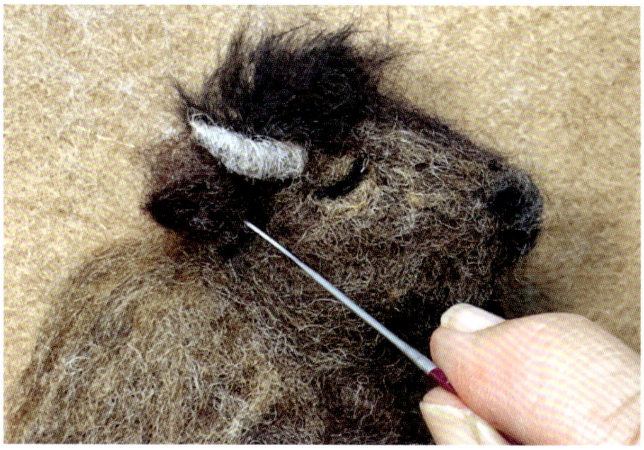

27. Felt in a curved strand of black wool for a closed eye. Then fold two pieces of dark brown wool into small rounds for ears and felt both sides. Attach behind the horns.

28. Create a tail by taking a length of dark brown top wool and rolling medium brown around it as shown. Felt all sides and trim the long hair. Attach to the back of the bison. You can use the hairspray/water mixture to texture the tail, mane, and beard (see page 16).

29. Now the bison is ready to roam or sleep!

LITTLE MOOSE

DIFFICULTY: Beginner–Intermediate

Moose embody the spirit of the Northwoods: Untamed, raw, and majestic. Encountering a moose on a trail feels almost sacred, a thrilling reminder of nature's grandeur. I've crossed paths with moose in many national parks, but an unforgettable moment was in Denali National Park along the Nenana River. I watched as a moose stepped into the river, was swept by the current, and emerged on the opposite bank near me. It paused, meeting my gaze, and for a few quiet seconds, we shared a wordless connection before it wandered into the trees. That day, I felt linked to something immense and wild. Moose inhabit diverse landscapes across the U.S., from the wetlands of Grand Teton and the river valleys of Yellowstone to the alpine meadows of Rocky Mountain, the coastal forests of Acadia, and the remote wilderness of Isle Royale and Voyageurs. Each park offers unique habitats that sustain moose populations, making them an essential part of our national park ecosystems.

This little moose isn't quite so intimidating. This is a beginner–intermediate project and you will learn to create moose antlers out of felt. It would make a wonderful decoration with a Northwoods vibe.

SUPPLIES

- Felting pad
- Felting needles
- Multi-needle felting tool
- Scissors
- White core wool
- Carded roving in the following colors:
  - Gray
  - Black
  - Brown
- Light tan wool felt cut into two 3" (7.6cm) squares
- 20-gauge wire
- 22-gauge wire
- Craft glue
- Flat-nosed pliers
- Little Moose templates, page 115

Antlers

1. Cut a 4¾" (12.1cm) piece of 22-gauge wire. Bend into a loose V shape, coat with glue, and wrap with wool, then fold the felt squares over the wire as pictured.

2. Felt the wool felt together vigorously until both sides are securely attached.

3. Coat each side of both antlers with a 50/50 mixture of craft glue and water and let it dry thoroughly while you work on the moose body.

4. When it's dry, use the template from page 115 and small sharp scissors to cut the felt into shape. You can add a little more glue/water mixture to the tips if the felt separates.

5. The antlers are ready.

Moose

1. Cut a 5½" (14cm) piece of 22-gauge wire, bend the wire at the nose, glue, and wrap with core wool, leaving ½" (1.2cm) uncovered for the tail.

2. Wrap another layer of wool around the body and felt into place.

3. Cut two pieces of 20-gauge wire, 9½" (24.1cm) and 10" (25.4cm). Insert the shorter piece for the front legs as pictured, and the longer piece for the back legs. Felt in a round of wool at the top of the back, over the front legs, for a hump.

4. Bend back the ends of the legs and wrap them with core wool from the bottom to the top. (See Wrapping the Wire on page 11.) With the flat-nosed plier, bend each of the hooves forward. Bend the back legs as shown in the picture and the template on page 115.

5. Take a small piece of gray wool and wrap the hooves. Then felt in place.

6. Wrap each of the legs with brown wool from the knee up. Add extra wool on the back thighs for thickness and felt in.

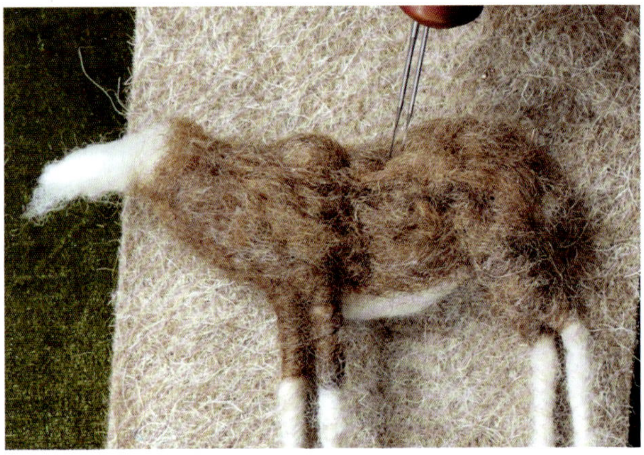

7. Add a layer of brown wool across the body from the front to the back and felt in place. Leave the tummy white.

8. Glue and wrap the little tail. Felt in a small piece of wool vertically down the tail.

9. Continue to wrap the entire head with brown wool and felt in place. Place the antlers and wrap a length of wool, then crisscross over the antlers to secure. Felt vigorously.

10. Create two tiny roundish ears and felt until solid, then place behind the antlers. (See page 14 for how to make and attach ears.)

11. Roll two oval balls and felt into the muzzle for nostrils. Felt in a strand of black underneath for a mouth. Then felt the end of the muzzle repeatedly to create the moose's unique, curved downward nose shape.

12. Take a small swatch of brown wool to felt in a tiny fluff of beard. (See page 15 for fluff.) Felt in a small, oval black eye and add eye lights.

13. Your moose is now finished!

SOARING EAGLE

DIFFICULTY: Intermediate

What an unforgettable moment to spot a bald eagle soaring overhead! With its massive wingspan, striking white head, and white tail, it's impossible to confuse this majestic bird with any other. The bald eagle has been the national symbol of the United States since 1782 and has held deep spiritual significance for Indigenous peoples for centuries, representing strength and a connection to the divine. Once on the brink of extinction, bald eagles have made a remarkable comeback thanks to conservation efforts and environmental protections. Today, they thrive in many wild places—including national parks. In Glacier National Park alone, they are among more than 260 bird species that call this breathtaking landscape home.

This intermediate bald eagle project will show you how to make a beak and simple wings. It includes a multi-step technique to create the bird's eyes. You can hang the eagle from a string for display.

SUPPLIES

- Felting pad
- Felting needles
- Multi-needle felting tool
- Scissors
- Core wool or white wool roving
- Carded roving in the following colors:
  - Dark brown
  - Light brown
  - Black
- Dark brown merino or alpaca top
- White merino wool
- Bright golden yellow top wool
- 20-gauge copper wire
- 24-gauge wire
- Craft glue
- Flat-nosed pliers
- Hair straightening iron or mini craft iron
- Hairspray/water mix

1. Starting with the wings, cut two 4" (10.2cm) lengths of 24-gauge wire, glue, and wrap a thin layer of brown wool, leaving ¾" (1.9cm) uncovered. Place the wire in the center of a thick 4½" (11.4cm) swatch of dark brown wool.

2. Fold the wool over the wire and felt together to create a wing shape.

3. Felt in some merino or alpaca top wool along the outer end and along the bottom of the wing by laying it down, felting in, and folding back (the same way as adding fur on page 15).

4. Trim along the bottom of the wing.

5. Flatten the wing with a hair straightener, or iron it.

6. Spray the wing with a hairspray/water mix and create a mirror version for the second wing. Set the wings aside.

7. Cut a 4½" (11.4cm) wire, glue the end, and fold back ½" (1.2cm). Glue and wrap the beak with yellow wool. Apply more glue to the beak and wrap more wool, leaving the end narrow. Then wrap the first layer of core wool on the head and body and felt in.

8. Start shaping the body by felting in wool thicker at the shoulders and tapered at the tail.

9. Wrap and felt in additional wool around the head and neck as pictured.

10. Add a swatch of wool across the top of the head to widen it.

11. Use needle-nose pliers to carefully bend down the very tip of the beak.

12. Fold over a piece of merino wool into a fan shape and felt it together lightly.

13. Felt the loose end into the back of the bird.

14. Spray the tail with the hairspray/water mix and fan and flatten it with your fingers.

15. Cover the body by felting in dark brown wool from the neck to the tail.

16. Add a wisp of light brown to the chest area.

17. Felt in white merino wool over the head from the beak to the neck, leaving the loose ends free.

18. Trim the bottom of the white merino.

19. With your felting needle, comb and felt in the bottom edge of the white head for a feathered look.

20. Felt in an elongated eye shape with black wool.

21. Felt in a small ball of yellow wool.

22. Add a small ball of black to the top of the eye and felt a line of black on top to define it. Add eye lights. Then felt in a line of yellow around the top and bottom of the beak to blend it into the head.

23. Attach the wings by inserting wire into the bird as shown.

24. Felt in the bottom of the wing firmly on both the front and back of the wing until it's secure. Repeat on the other side.

25. Take two small lengths of yellow and felt the centers into the bottom of the bird for claws.

26. Insert a string from the top of the eagle, behind the white head, down to the bottom, and back up again, and it is ready to fly. Balancing the bird can be tricky, but it works better with the wings flat out.

TRUMPETER SWAN AND CYGNET

DIFFICULTY: Intermediate

When I worked at Yellowstone National Park, a friend led me to a quiet lake where I saw a trumpeter swan for the first time. Its elegance and sheer size left me in awe. Trumpeter swans are the largest waterfowl in North America and the heaviest native bird, stretching over 5 feet (1.5m) in length. I didn't realize then how rare that sighting was—these swans have been declining in Yellowstone since the 1960s, though restoration efforts continue. Yellowstone, America's first national park, is home to an incredible array of wildlife, from grizzly bears to wolves, and its vast lakes and rivers provide critical habitat for species like the trumpeter swan. Nearby Grand Teton National Park also offers a sanctuary for these magnificent birds, along with moose, elk, and countless other species. Together, these parks form part of the Greater Yellowstone Ecosystem, one of the largest nearly intact temperate ecosystems on Earth, making them vital for conservation and unforgettable for visitors.

You can create your own, much more diminutive swan, with a little cygnet as well. This intermediate project will teach you how to create a swan beak and will have you working on a tiny scale with the cygnet.

SUPPLIES

- Felting pad
- Felting needles
- Multi-needle felting tool
- Scissors
- White core wool or white carded roving
- White merino wool
- Dark gray top wool
- Light pink top wool
- Carded roving in the following colors:
  - Black
  - Light gray
- 24-gauge wire
- Craft glue
- Flat needle-nose pliers
- Hairspray/water mixture
- Trumpeter Swan and Cygnet template (page 116)

Swan

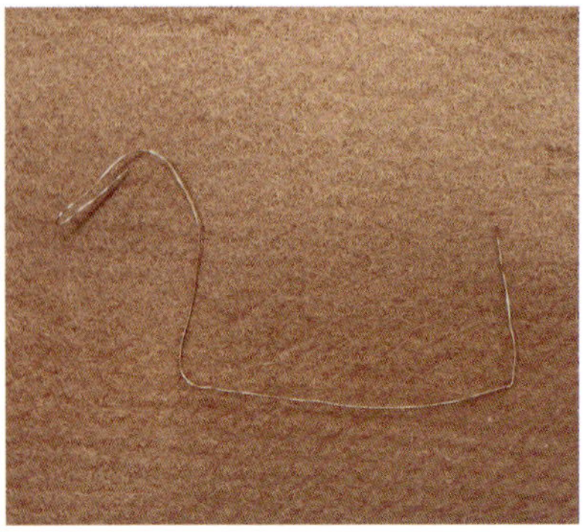

1. Cut a 13" (33cm) length of 24-gauge wire and bend into a swan shape as in the template (page 116) and the photo. Bend back a curved shape of 1" (2.5cm) for the beak.

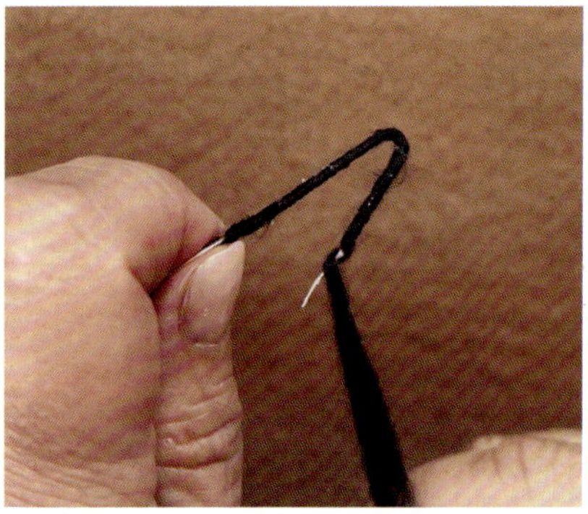

2. Glue the beak area and take a strand of dark gray wool and cover the beak wire. Then, wrap the wool around the beak and lightly felt in place.

3. Wrap the swan in wool, making sure to leave the extra wire at the end uncovered.

4. Wrap and felt wool around the head to create an oval shape. Then felt in two small rounds of wool on the lower sides of the head.

5. Start wrapping the body with more wool and felting in. Add more wool in the center to create an oval shape with the body.

6. Felt in a swatch of wool to the sides of the body to create a rounded oval shape. Then felt in a swatch of wool to the top of the swan to create a slight hump.

7. Once you're happy with the length of the swan, cut off the excess wire and fold under the body.

8. Wrap a thin layer of merino wool around the neck.

9. Take a length of merino wool and lay it vertically down the neck. Felt into place on all sides.

10. Start covering the head by felting in merino wool from the beak to the back of the head.

11. Poke in the area halfway from the beak to the back of the head to create an eye indentation.

12. Take a strand of gray wool and create a U shape that goes from above the beak to the eye indentations, and felt in.

13. Felt in another strand from the eye to underneath the beak.

14. Roll a piece of gray wool and felt in under the curve and over the beak about two-thirds of the way.

15. Felt in more gray wool to fill in the area between the eyes and the beak. Wrap the rest of the beak in another thin layer of wool and felt in place.

16. Flatten the end of the beak by squeeing with flat-nosed pliers. Spray with a hairspray/water mixture to help flatten.

17. Roll a small ball of black wool for the eye and felt in place. Felt in a tiny strand of white wool at the inner eye and cut off excess. Felt in eye lights and the head is done.

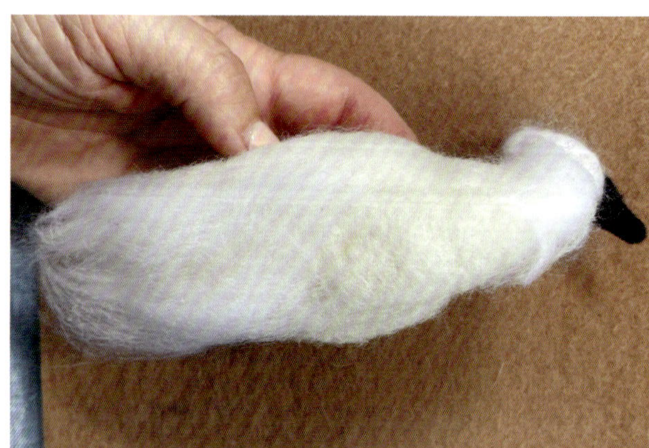

18. Start to cover the body with merino wool by laying swatches from the front to the back. Felt in vigorously on the bottom of the swan so it sits flat.

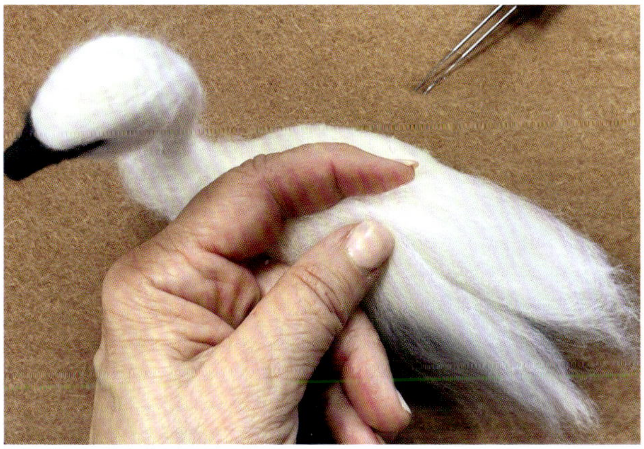

19. Felt merino wool into the back and sides, but leave the ends loose.

20. Finish felting in merino along the entire body.

21. Take two thick lengths of merino wool and felt lightly along the middle, leavening the ends loose.

22. Felt in a loose end just under the start of the hump, and then fold back over the swan.

23. Felt the wing in along the front and the bottom, leaving the back and the top loose. Repeat on the other side.

24. Trim off any feathers that are too long, then lightly spray the wings and the tail with the hairspray/water mixture to create texture. Comb out the ends with your needle.

Cygnet

1. Cut a 3" (7.6cm) piece of 24-gauge wire and shape like the adult swan, but make a shorter neck. Cover the beak with pink wool, and then continue to wrap with white merino wool. (Since the cygnet is so small, it is better to use merino wool for the entire body.)

2. Wrap the wool to create the oval shape of the head, then felt in white merino from the front to the back.

3. Take a round of wool and felt in a hump.

4. Felt in merino wool from the front to the back and cut off the excess.

TIP

Reading glasses can be very helpful when working on tiny projects.

5. Felt the centers of two tiny swatches of merino wool.

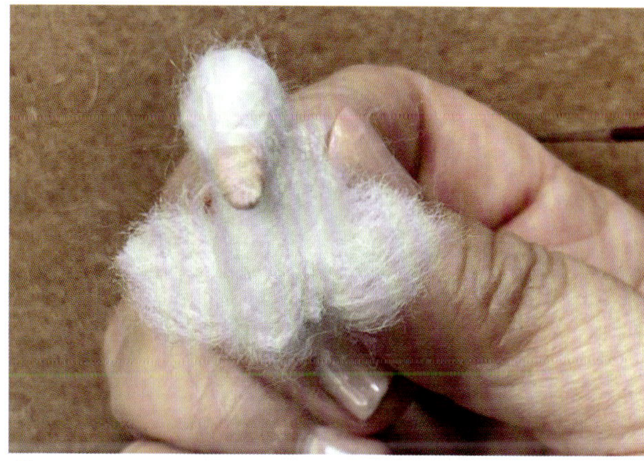

6. Felt in the wings and cut off the excess.

7. Felt in light gray wool along the top of the head, the back, and the front of the wings.

8. Felt in tiny black eyes with eye lights.

9. Place the cygnet on the back of the swan, and mom and baby are ready for a swim! (Not really, please don't place in water.)

GRIZZLY BEAR CUB

DIFFICULTY: Intermediate

I've always adored bears and feel fortunate to have seen grizzlies—often called brown bears—in both Yellowstone and Denali National Parks. These powerful animals also roam Glacier National Park, where rugged mountains and pristine valleys provide critical habitat. Historically, grizzlies ranged from Alaska down into Mexico and east across the Great Plains, but their numbers plummeted due to hunting and habitat loss. Today, they remain abundant in Alaska, while in the lower 48 states they are listed as Threatened under the Endangered Species Act. Most populations are now confined to parts of Montana, Wyoming, Idaho, and Washington, with Yellowstone and Glacier serving as strongholds for their survival. These parks are part of vast ecosystems—Yellowstone is the heart of the Greater Yellowstone Ecosystem, and Glacier anchors the Crown of the Continent—both essential for preserving biodiversity and offering visitors a rare chance to witness these iconic animals in the wild.

This grizzly cub is an intermediate project, but it's also suitable for a beginner with some experience. Created on a continuous wire frame, the cub can be posed sitting, standing, or walking. While this design is a brown bear, you may also choose to make him all white for a polar bear cub or dark brown/ black for a black bear. Any way you make him, he's certain to be delightful in any woodland display.

SUPPLIES

- Felting pad
- Felting needles
- Multi-needle felting tool
- Scissors
- Core wool or white carded roving
- Carded wool roving in the following colors:
  - Light golden brown
  - Medium brown
  - Tan
  - Black
- 26" (66cm) 22-gauge copper wire
- Craft glue
- Flat-nosed pliers
- Grizzly Bear Cub template (page 116)

1. Bend the copper wire into a frame by starting at the head and going down to create two even legs, and up to the shoulders to create two even arms. Follow the template on page 116. Squeeze the paws closed with the pliers.

2. Apply glue to the paws and the nose and wrap wool around the entire frame. Wrap extra bulk around the middle.

3. Continue to felt in extra wool around the middle, and add a swatch to the back bottom.

4. Roll a piece of wool and add it to the tummy.

5. Roll a piece of tan wool about halfway up the face for the muzzle and felt it in place.

6. Wrap and felt the rest of the head with wool and wrap the neck.

7. To fill out the head, roll a swatch of wool, felt it, and add it to the top of the head and felt in place.

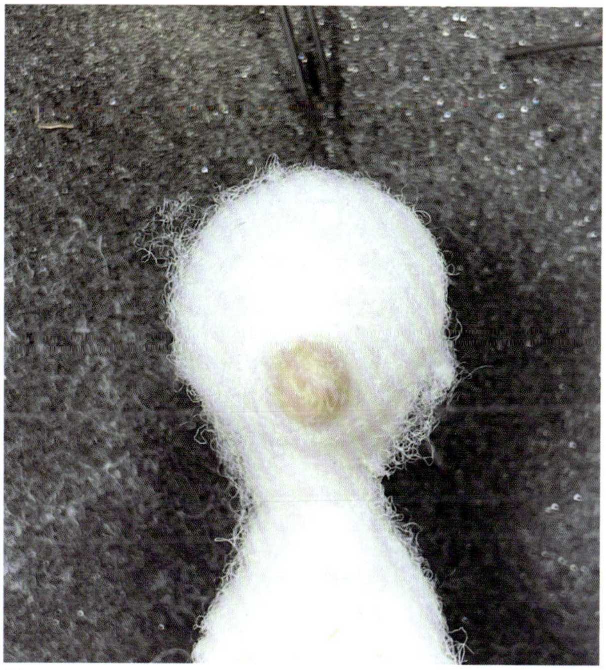

8. Wrap extra wool around the head and felt in to create a head that is wider at the top.

9. Wrap another small layer of tan wool around the snout, and then felt in light golden wool underneath.

10. Continue to cover the head, directing wool strands from the muzzle to the back of the head and felting in.

11. To create the shape of the muzzle, fold and felt a piece of tan wool to create a squared edge, leaving the other end loose.

12. Place the square on the underside of the muzzle and felt in. Bring the loose fiber over the muzzle and felt into place.

13. Create two ears by folding and felting small lengths of wool. Felt a medium brown oval in the center.

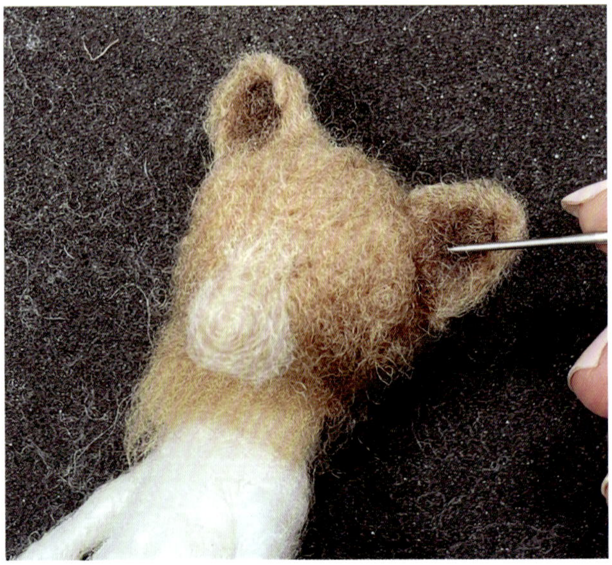

14. Position the ears on the far sides of the head and felt in place as described on page 14.

15. Using medium brown wool, wrap halfway down the legs and feet, as well as the arms, and felt in place.

16. Felt the feet vigorously on the top and bottom to flatten them.

17. Felt in brown wool vertically down the arms and legs. (See Adding Bulk and Defining the Shape on page 12.) Wrap the tops of the legs and arms with golden brown wool.

18. Felt in golden wool over the brown, leaving hands and feet brown. Continue to felt wool over the legs and arms and over the body until it is the desired thickness.

19. Fold and felt a small piece of wool for a tail and attach.

20. Create a chevron with white wool by felting a swatch of white wool into a slight V shape. See Techniques (page 15) for adding fluff.

21. Roll an oval-shaped nose with black wool and felt into place.

22. Place a small strand of gray or brown under the nose and felt in a mouth. (See page 13.)

23. Roll two small round black balls and felt in on either side of the muzzle. Felt in eye lights.

24. Felt in a tiny swatch of gray or brown above the nose. Your grizzly bear is ready to pose!

CUTE PIKA

DIFFICULTY: Intermediate–Advanced

You may have never seen—or even heard of—this adorable little creature: the American pika. These tiny mammals live in alpine terrain, high in the mountains among rocky slopes above the tree line. Despite their rugged habitat, pikas are highly sensitive to heat and vulnerable to extreme weather. A close relative of the rabbit, they spend summers gathering vegetation to store for winter survival. According to the National Park Service, the pika is considered an indicator species for detecting the effects of climate change in mountainous regions, as warming temperatures threaten their ability to thrive. Researchers have already observed a decline in their range. You can find pikas in Rocky Mountain National Park and other alpine parks like Yosemite, Yellowstone, and Glacier—places that protect the high-elevation ecosystems these animals depend on. These parks not only offer stunning scenery but also serve as critical refuges for species uniquely adapted to life above the tree line.

This pika is an intermediate–advanced project. Creating this will give you the skills necessary for similar species such as mice and rabbits. The life-size pika would be fittingly displayed on a rock.

SUPPLIES

- Felting pad
- Felting needles
- Multi-needle felting tool
- Scissors
- White core wool
- Carded roving in the following colors:
  - Light gray-brown
  - Dark gray-brown
  - Dark brown
  - Black
- White merino top wool
- 22-gauge wire
- White horsehair
- Sewing needle
- Craft glue
- Awl
- Brown fine-tipped alcohol pen
- Stem of dried or silk flower or grass.

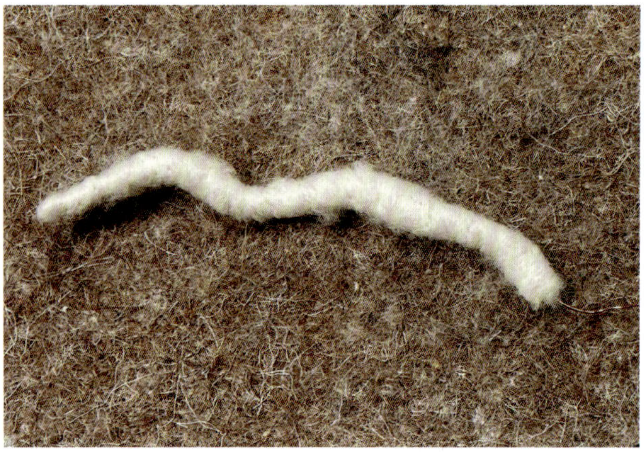

1. Cut a 6½" (16.5cm) length of wire, bend over the front and glue, and then wrap from top to bottom.

2. Start building the face by wrapping more wool and felting in, then adding rounds of wool for the cheeks.

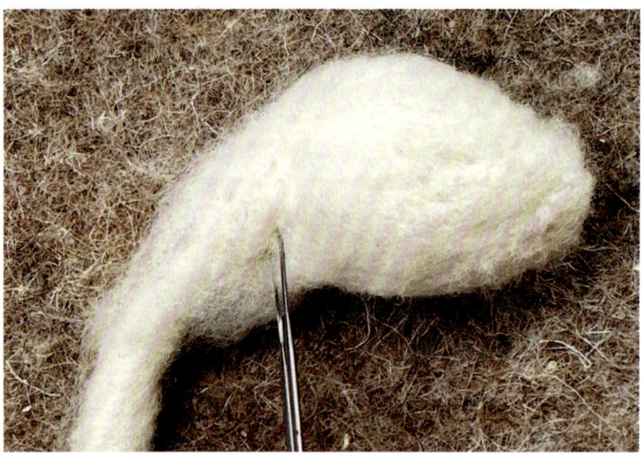

3. Felt in extra wool across the nose from front to back. Felt extra wool across the top of the head to create a head shape.

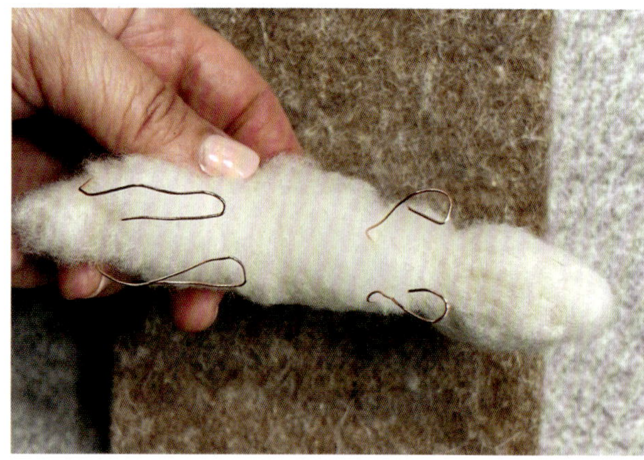

4. Wrap and felt in two more layers of wool to the body. Insert two lengths of wire as shown for the legs: 5½" (14cm) in the front and 6" (15.2cm) in back. Fold back the legs.

5. Create rounds of wool and felt in place for the haunches. Felt in additional wool along the back to create a rounded shape.

6. Wrap all the legs from top to bottom as described on page 12.

7. Create thicker, flatter legs by folding swatches of wool and felting them slightly, then felting them onto the front of the legs. Fold over the remaining wool and felt into the back of the legs. Take swatches of white merino wool and felt vertically over all the legs. Then felt in a swatch of merino wool along the underside of the pika.

8. Create a little nose of core wool and felt in place to create a more pointed face shape.

9. Felt in merino wool from the neck to the top of the head and felt in; then felt in a swatch across the nose.

10. Start covering the head with light brown-gray wool by laying across the face and leaving the muzzle white.

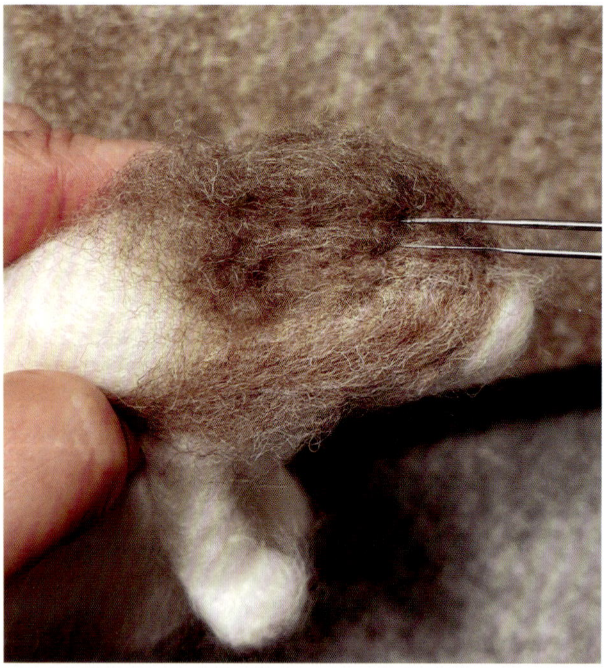

11. Cover all the head with light brown-gray wool and felt in. Take a swatch of darker wool and felt in along the top of the head from the nose to the back.

12. Use the same darker wool to shape a triangle, then felt it into the nose.

13. Take a strand of dark brown wool and line the nose. Felt in a line under the nose and felt another small strand for a mouth as pictured.

14. Fold core wool into rounded ears (see page 14) and felt in darker brown-gray wool into the centers. Attach the ears by felting into the head.

15. Felt vigorously from the nose to the center of the head to create indentations for the eyes.

16. Create a tapered round of dark brown/black wool and felt into place for an eye.

17. Felt in eye lights, and then felt in a small swatch of the lighter brown-gray wool above the eye and cut off excess.

18. Cover the rest of the body by felting the lighter brown-gray wool along the bottom and the darker shade over the back on top.

19. Add fluff with the merino wool under the neck and across the chest as described on page 15.

20. Felt in four strands of brown lines to define paws and cut off extra length of strands.

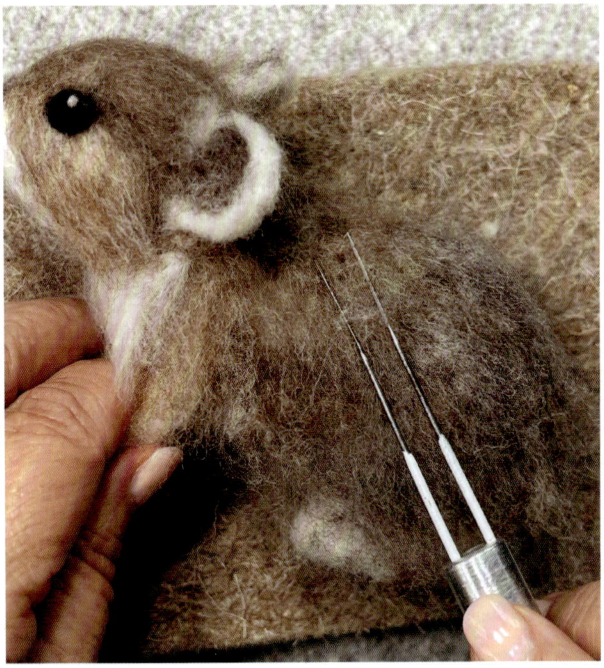

21. Pull out and comb the coat with a reverse-felting needle to create a furry look. See page 16.

22. Use a brown, fine-tipped alcohol pen to create two lines of whisker freckles. You may want to practice this first on a wool ball.

23. Create whiskers with white horsehair by threading the horsehair into a sewing needle, tying a knot in the middle, and pulling through. (See Arctic Seal Pup tutorial on page 44.)

24. Carefully insert an awl at the outer edge of the mouth from one side to the other to create a hole.

25. Insert the stem.

26. Your pika is ready for display!

SEQUOIA TREES AND FOX WOOL PAINTING

DIFFICULTY: Advanced

Sequoia National Park was the first national park I ever worked in, and it will always hold a special place in my heart. This painting is a tribute to the awe-inspiring beauty of the giant Sequoia trees—some of the largest and oldest living organisms on Earth, reaching heights of over 250 feet and surviving for more than 3,000 years—and to one of the most unforgettable summers of my life. While living in the park, I encountered many black bears, a common sight in this region, but never saw a fox; however, Sequoia is home to the elusive Sierra Nevada red fox, an endangered subspecies adapted to high elevations. These foxes are smaller than typical red foxes and have a striking golden-red coat that helps them blend into their alpine environment, and sadly, fewer than 40 individuals are estimated to remain in the wild. National parks like Sequoia are sanctuaries for biodiversity and natural wonders, protecting ecosystems, providing habitat for rare species, and offering people the chance to experience landscapes that have remained largely unchanged for millennia—a reminder of why conservation matters and why these places are worth preserving for future generations.

This wool painting is an advanced project. It will build on the skills of the Howling Wolf Starry Night Wool Painting (page 36) and the skills used in the needle-felted animals. It requires many light layers of wool to create the painterly effect. The little fox uses the various techniques for creating animal physiques, and the miniature is especially challenging.

SUPPLIES

- Large felting pad to accommodate 12" x 16" (30.5 x 40.6cm)
- Small felting pad
- Multi-needle tool with two fine needles
- Scissors
- Piece of felt cut into 12" x 16" (30.5 x 40.6cm)
- Top wool in the following colors:
  - Light blue
  - Bright white
  - Medium brown
  - Red-brown
  - Light brown or medium tan
  - Light tan
  - Leaf green
  - Light green
- Carded roving in the following colors:
  - Dark green
  - Very light gray
  - Black
  - Gold-red
  - Gray
  - Bright white
- Iron
- Awl

1. Spread the light blue wool in very thin layers horizontally across the felt. Felt in well along the edges and lightly in the middle.

2. Iron the wool on a low setting so it is flattened.

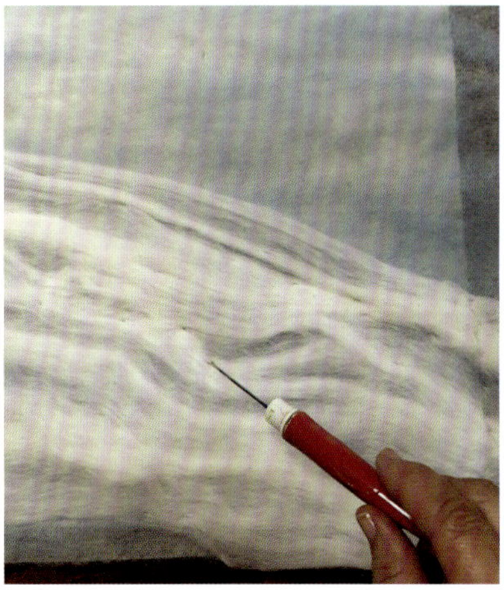

3. Lay a hill of white wool along the bottom as pictured. Felt along the edges and more lightly across the middle, leaving some blue streaks showing for texture.

TIP

It is a good idea to practice the techniques for making tree bark and greenery on a small piece of felt before you begin this project.

4. Start creating the trees by taking a length of medium brown wool. Spread it wider at the bottom and anchor with your hand. With your other hand, pull at the top of the tree to create a tapered tree. Start with a wider tree at the left side that starts closer to the bottom and a narrower tree at the right as shown.

5. Felt trees in place along the edges, keeping the tapered shape. Add a third tree as shown.

6. Cover all three trees with a very thin layer of reddish-brown wool.

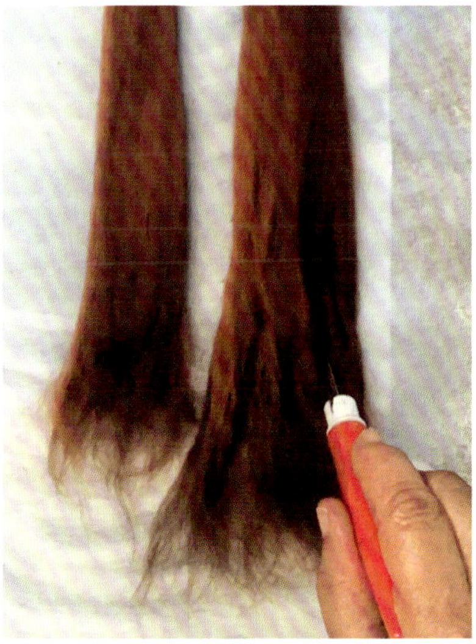

7. Add a very thin layer of the medium brown wool along the right side of the trees. Felt the layers into the trees by felting along the edges, and then felt in lines with your multi-needle tool to simulate bark.

8. Take a very thin length of the light brown and place it on top of a thin length of the red brown for distant trees. Felt in two distant trees as shown.

9. Take thin pieces of the light gray wool and place it between all the trees at the bottom half to create a fog.

10. Take very thin wispy lengths of dark green wool and drape them to look like pine tree branches. (Don't worry too much about the small trees as they will mostly be covered by the branches of the big trees.)

11. Separate small swatches of white carded roving to lay along the bottom of the big trees.

12. Take a length of white wool and cut small pieces of it to scatter along the bottom of the trees, and then felt in place.

13. Add a length of white wool for thicker snow along the bottom of the painting and felt in place.

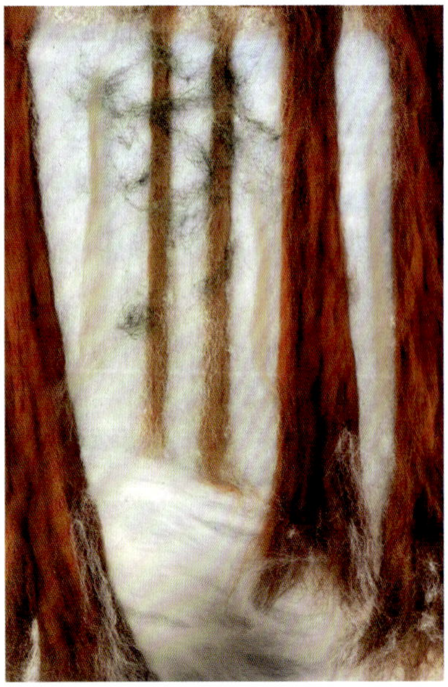

14. Take thin lengths of light tan wool to create ghost trees in the distance and felt in place.

15. Mix light green wool with a little dark green wool for small wisps along the ghost trees. (Again, most of this will be covered by the big branches.)

16. Add a few more dark green branches to the middle trees so it is clear that they are in front of the ghost trees

17. Blend a length of leaf green wool with dark green wool. Cut small pieces of the wool and arrange them for branches. Move the pieces around until you are satisfied, then felt in place.

18. Add branches in the same manner on the big tree, including a length of a hanging branch in front of the tree.

19. Take a thin length of brown wool and felt next to and behind the big tree for a baby tree.

20. Cut bits of the green wool mix and arrange over the tree trunk in a Christmas tree shape.

21. Use a small felting pad to create the fox. Roll two small rounds of wool, with one being the head and neck and the other being the rear. Connect with a 1" (2.5cm) length of wool for the body. Roll a tiny piece of wool and felt into the head for the muzzle. Then take thin lengths of black wool and create four legs by rolling the wool between your fingers. Felt into the fox. (The fox is loosely created on the pad and will be defined once it's on the painting.)

23. Cover the legs halfway with red-gold wool and lightly felt in place. Take a length of white wool and felt in for a tail.

22. Felt in a light layer of gold-red wool as shown. You can lightly lift the fox off the pad to make sure it's not getting felted into it.

24. Cover the tail with red-gold wool, leaving white at the end. Add a thin piece of gray wool along the tail and the back of the fox.

25. Roll a tiny black ball and felt in for the nose. (You can adjust this after it's on the painting.) Fold a small piece of black into a triangle for an ear and felt into the head. Felt in a tiny length of black wool for an eye.

26. Remove the fox carefully from the pad. An awl works well to lift the felted piece. Place it in the painting.

27. Start by felting the legs into the painting. The feet will be sunken into the snow. Then felt along the edges of the fox to define the shape. Be sure to felt the nose in place. You can leave the tail a little loose and swinging. You can felt in a tiny piece of light blue wool behind the end of the tail and under the head to make the white stand out.

28. Felt in a tiny line of black for the mouth. You can continue to tweak your fox until you are satisfied. And you may want to add or rearrange the tree branches.

29. Once you are satisfied, turn the painting over and felt in the loose wool to the back of the painting. You can display the painting in a shadow box frame or sew in a string for hanging.

CARIBOU/REINDEER

DIFFICULTY: Advanced

Caribou and reindeer are the same species—called caribou in North America and reindeer in Eurasia—and Alaska is the only U.S. state where wild caribou roam. Interestingly, Alaska also has domesticated herds of reindeer, which can make things a little confusing. One fun fact: Female reindeer keep their antlers year-round, while males shed theirs in the fall, meaning Santa's famous team was likely all females! Caribou are iconic animals of the Arctic and subarctic, perfectly adapted to cold environments with thick coats and large hooves for traveling across snow and tundra. If you take a bus tour deep into the wilderness of Denali National Park, one of Alaska's most breathtaking protected areas, you have a good chance of spotting caribou among its vast landscapes of mountains, glaciers, and boreal forests. National parks like Denali play a vital role in preserving these species and their habitats, offering visitors a rare opportunity to witness wildlife in its natural environment while safeguarding ecosystems for future generations.

This project is advanced. It includes a lesson on creating antlers and explores some finer detailing. This caribou could be the center of an exquisite Christmas display.

SUPPLIES

- Felting pad
- Thin felting pad
- Felting needles
- Multi-needle felting tool
- Scissors
- Core wool
- Carded roving in the following colors:
  - White
  - Dark brown
  - Medium brown
  - Black
- Merino or top wool in the following colors:
  - Tan
  - White
- 22-gauge copper wire
- 18-gauge copper wire
- 24-gauge wire
- Craft glue
- Glue and water mixture or fabric stiffener/water mixture
- Hairspray/water mix
- Flat-nosed pliers
- Awl
- Brown alcohol pen or fabric paint
- Caribou/Reindeer templates, page 117

1. Start with a 30" (76.2cm) length of 24-gauge wire and begin to bend into the antler shape in the template on page 117. Start at the middle of the wire and fold a small antler. (The other side of the antler is already done in this photo.)

2. Continue to fold a small double antler.

3. Create the top double antler and twist the wire back down to the bottom. There should be a small length of wire left at the bottom. Repeat on the other side, ensuring that both sides match.

4. Pinch the antler ends closed with flat-nosed pliers.

5. Coat the antler with glue and then take a long thin piece of tan merino wool and start to wrap the antler from the bottom moving upwards.Wrap the entire antler and add extra lengths of wool and glue along the antler length to thicken it. The antler should look as pictured.

6. Coat the antler with a glue/water mixture and spread evenly over the antlers to stiffen. Roll the ends between your fingers or press with flat-nosed pliers to make them pointy.

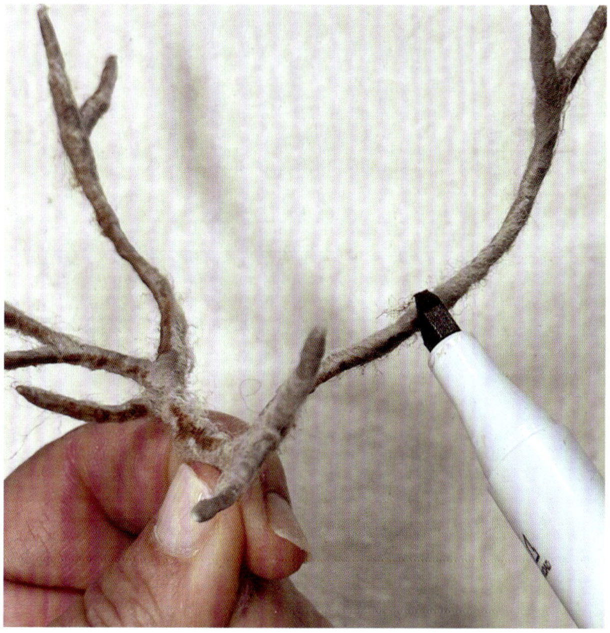

7. Color the outer side of the antlers with a medium brown alcohol pen. You do not have to wait for the glue to dry completely. Alternatively, you can shade the outside of the antlers with fabric paint.

8. Set the antlers aside. Cut two pieces of 22-gauge wire for the armature: One 8½" (21.6cm) and the other 7½" (19.1cm). Glue the ends of the wire and wrap both with core wool. Bend the longer piece into the head and the back, and shape leaving uncovered wire for the tail. Bend the smaller piece over the back of the head around to the tail, and wrap the remainder over the back as pictured.

9. Wrap the core wool around the head and around the entire body armature and felt into place.

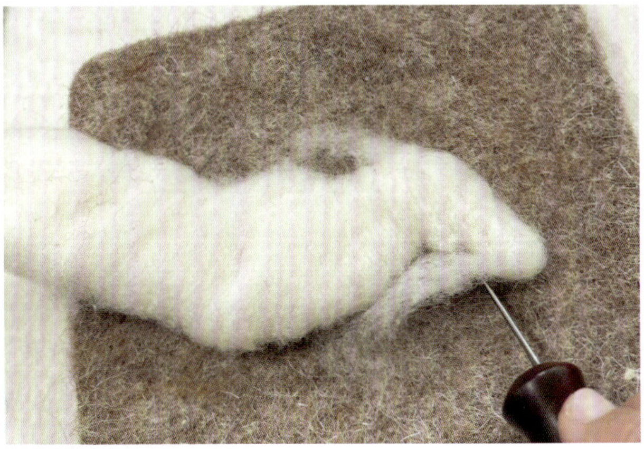

10. Begin to create the head shape by felting a swatch of wool from the neck over the muzzle and the top of the head.

11. Add a swatch of wool across the top of the head to widen it. Then add more wool across the eye area to create the head that is wider in the back than toward the muzzle.

12. Start adding bulk to the body by rolling a swatch of wool and felting in along the bottom and the side of the belly on both sides. Then roll a swatch of wool and felt in place for a hump behind the neck.

13. Wrap the body with another coat of core wool and felt in. Felt in more wool to create a chest, and then felt in rounds of wool at the hips.

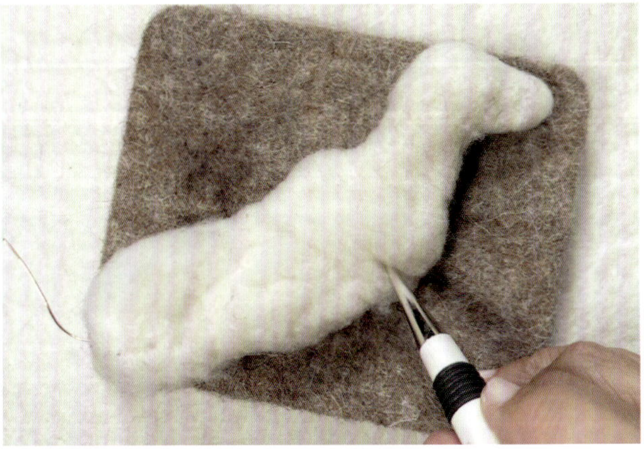

14. Use an awl to create a hole for the legs under the hump and under the hips.

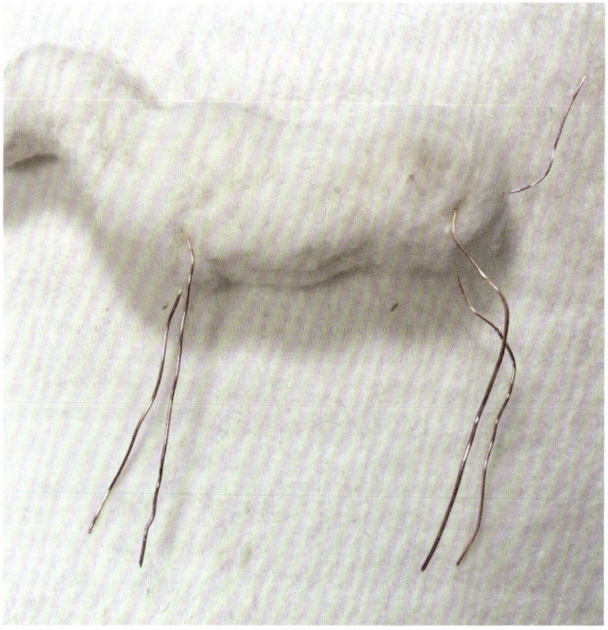

15. Cut your 18-gauge wire into one 8" (20.3cm) and one 9" (22.9cm) piece. Run the shorter piece through the front and the longer through the back.

16. Bend back the bottom of the legs and apply glue. Then wrap medium brown wool from the top to the bottom of the legs and then back up to the top.

17. Bend the hooves forward slightly with flat-nosed pliers. Ensure the legs are even and the caribou can stand.

18. Add glue to the hooves and then roll a strand of black around each hoof, wrapping less wool toward the tip for a taper. Felt in place and then flatten the ends with flat-nosed pliers.

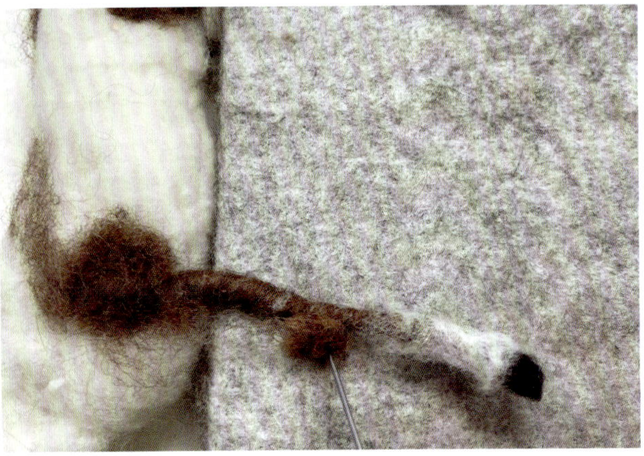

19. Straddle the caribou on a thin felting pad and wrap a small swatch of white wool at the top of the black hooves. Felt in on both sides. Then roll a small piece of wool and felt into place for a knee on the front leg.

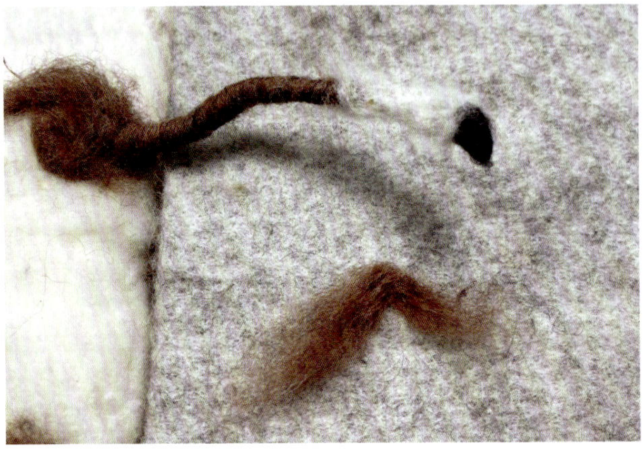

20. Bend a piece of wool and felt a right angle. Felt into place at the knee on back leg and then continue felting in lengths of wool from the top to the bottom, leaving some of the white exposed.

21. Felt in extra wool along the thigh.

22. Repeat, adding wool on all legs, and then turn over and fold the edges of the wool into the inside of the legs and felt in.

23. Felt in small lengths of wool on the inside of the legs to keep consistent texture. Add additional wool to the inner thigh.

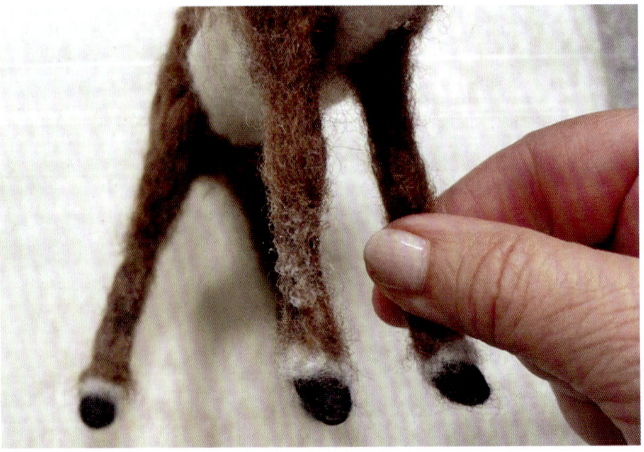

24. Spray the legs with the hairspray mixture and roll the bottoms of the legs between your fingers to make them thinner.

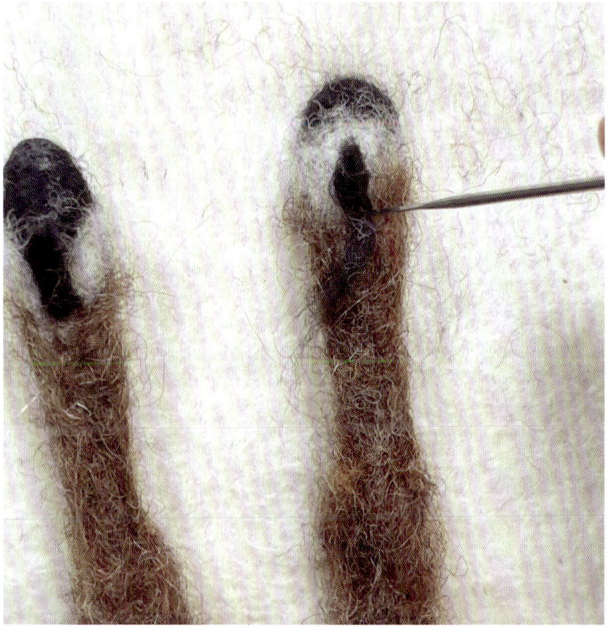

25. Take four thin strands of black wool, fold them over, felt them, and then roll them between your fingers. Felt them into place in the back of the hooves for a dewclaw.

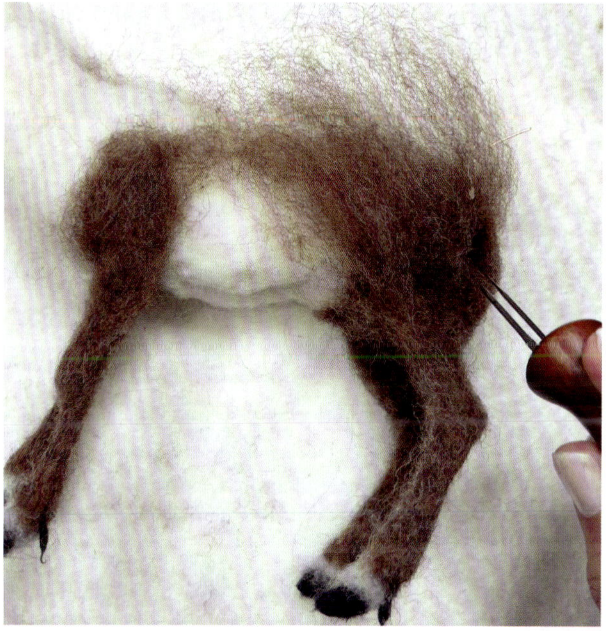

26. Felt brown wool into the body with strands running from front to back, stopping in front of the hump.

27. Add a swatch of white to the belly.

28. Glue the wire sticking out of the back and roll with white wool. Felt a swatch of wool horizontally across the tail, leaving the edges free. Felt in a little brown swatch to blend the body to the tail. Felt white wool into the hind around the tail, creating a heart shape.

29. Felt in a very thin coat of brown around the neck. Cover the brown with a coat of white, creating a speckled white, and trim the edges.

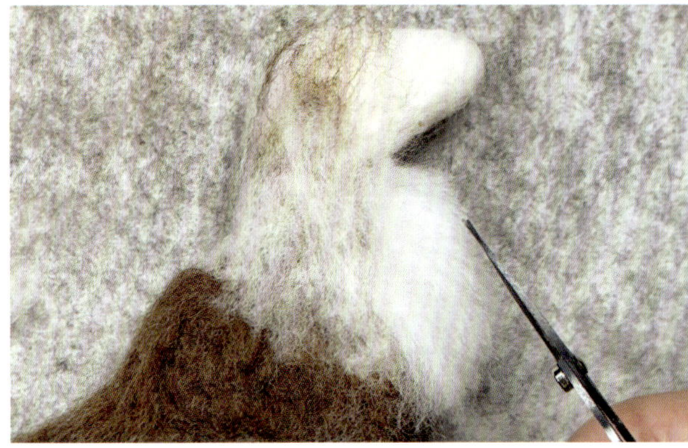

30. Felt in three or more layers of white merino for fluff as explained on page 15. Trim the fur and brush it out lightly with your felting needle. Add two very thin strands of brown under the neck.

31. Felt in brown wool from the front to the back of the head, leaving the muzzle uncovered.

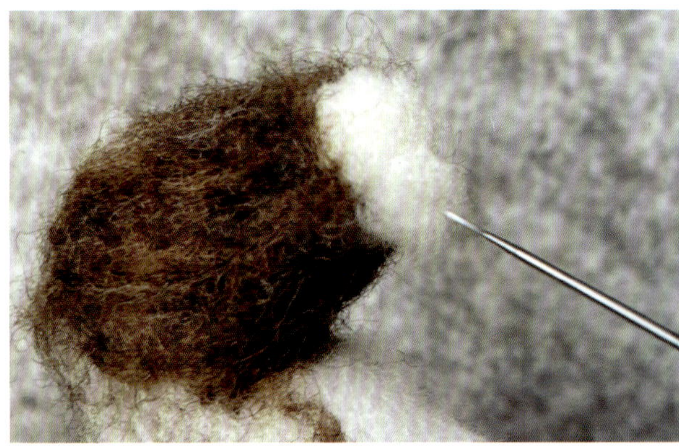

32. Take a small round of white wool and felt in at the chin.

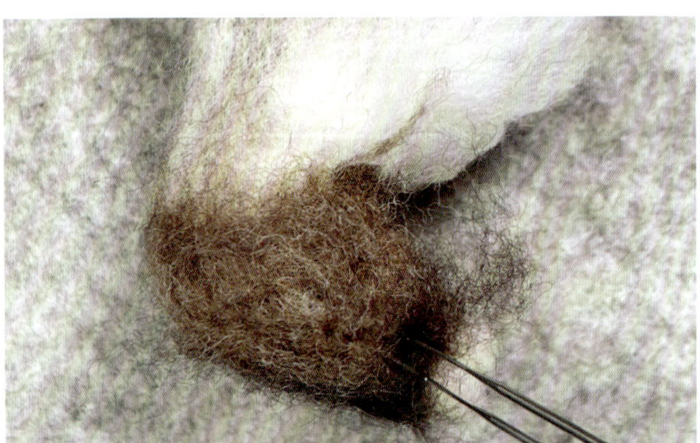

33. Felt in a small piece of darker brown above the muzzle, and then felt the darker brown along the sides of the muzzle.

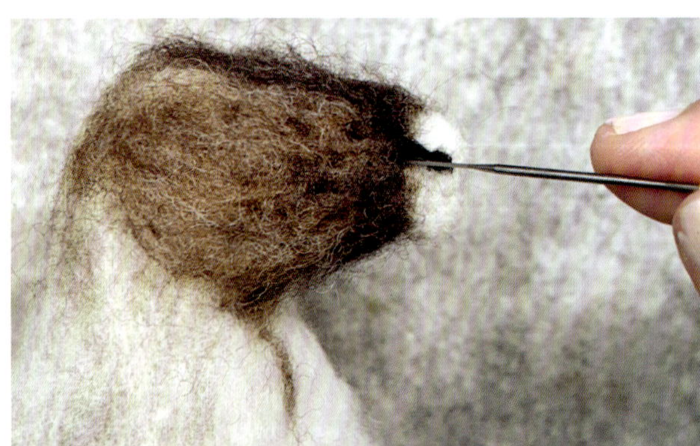

34. Roll two small pieces of black wool into an elongated oval and felt in the nostril as pictured. Felt a strand of dark brown into the space between the muzzle and where the chin was added and back to the end of the white for the mouth. Add a very thin piece of brown wool between the nostrils.

35. Create the eye by felting in a black oval. Felt a thin strand of white wool under the eye and then another strand above the eye. Cut off excess white. Take a thin strand of black and felt in above the eye, felting the strand in a downward direction in front of the eye. Add eye lights.

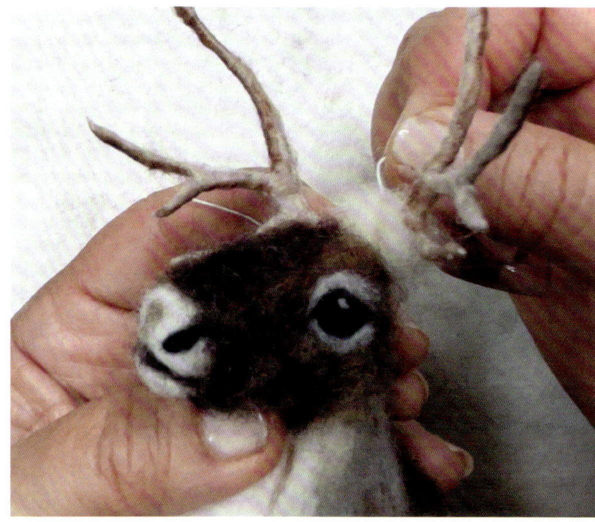

36. To attach the antlers, roll a little white wool around the middle of the antlers, so you can felt them in place. Center the antlers behind the eyes and push the extra uncovered wire on the antlers through the head, with the left wire going through to the right and vice versa. Roll the excess wire around the very bottom of the antler to secure, and then clip off the end. Felt a swatch of white wool over the antlers.

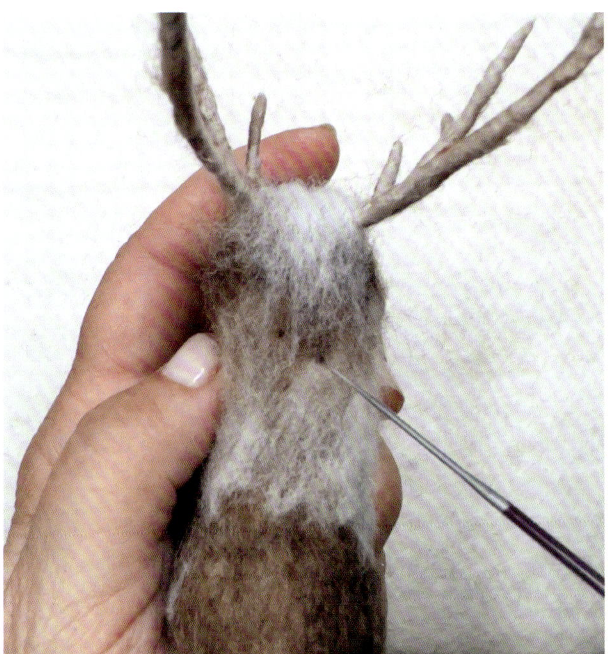

37. Felt in more white down from the top of the head to blend into the neck.

38. Create the ears by folding two triangles of dark brown wool and felting, then adding a swatch of medium brown and felt in. Turn the ears over and felt in a wisp of white and more dark brown in the center.

39. Attach the ears as described on page 15, slightly behind the antlers.

40. You can spray the fur with the hairspray mixture, arrange the antlers, and lift one of the legs if you like. Now your caribou is ready to display!

Templates

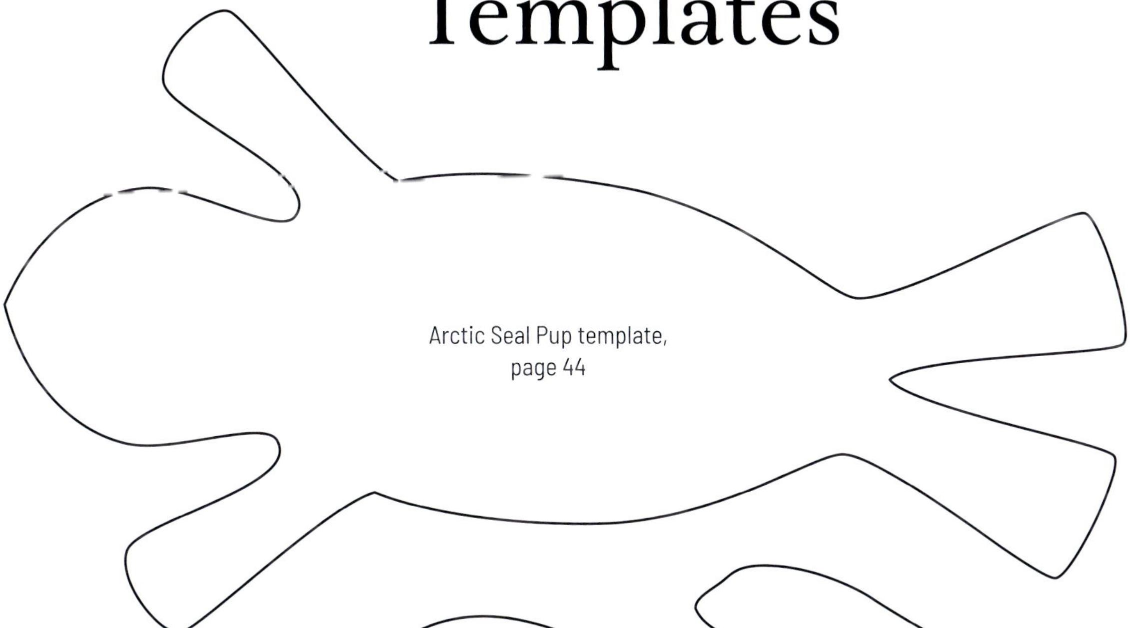
Arctic Seal Pup template,
page 44

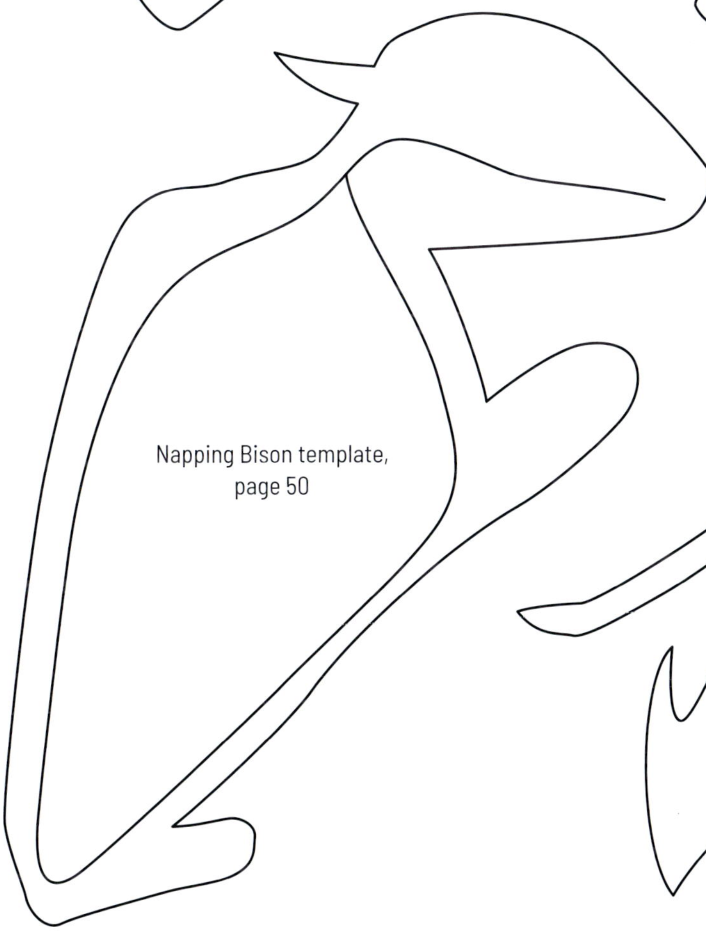
Napping Bison template,
page 50

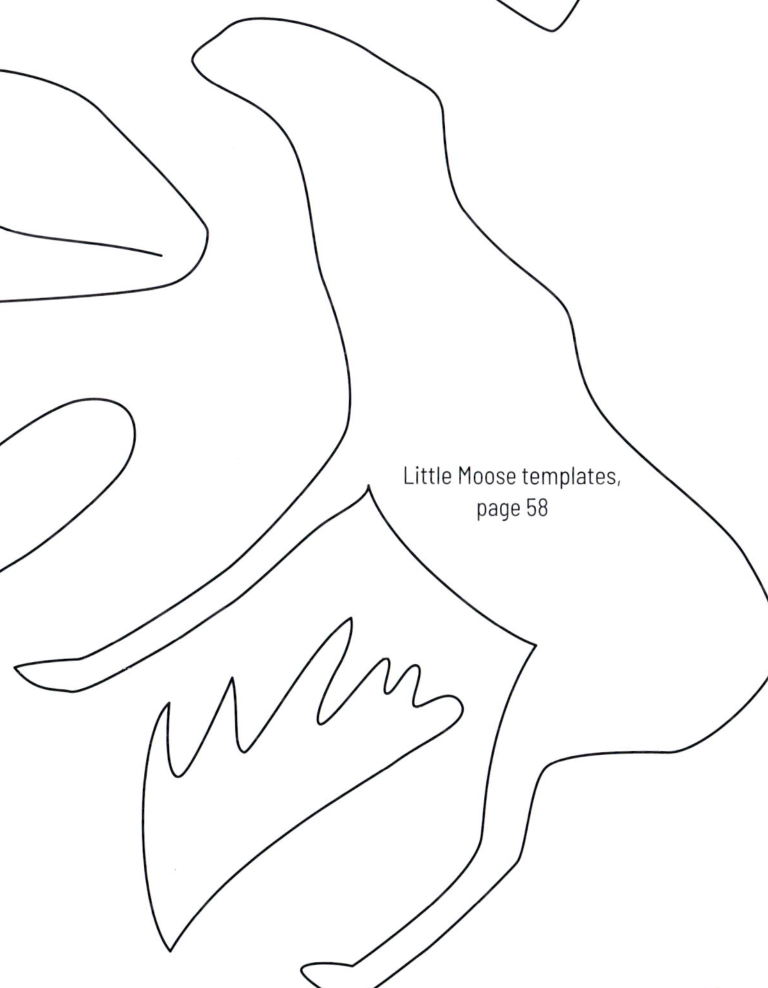
Little Moose templates,
page 58

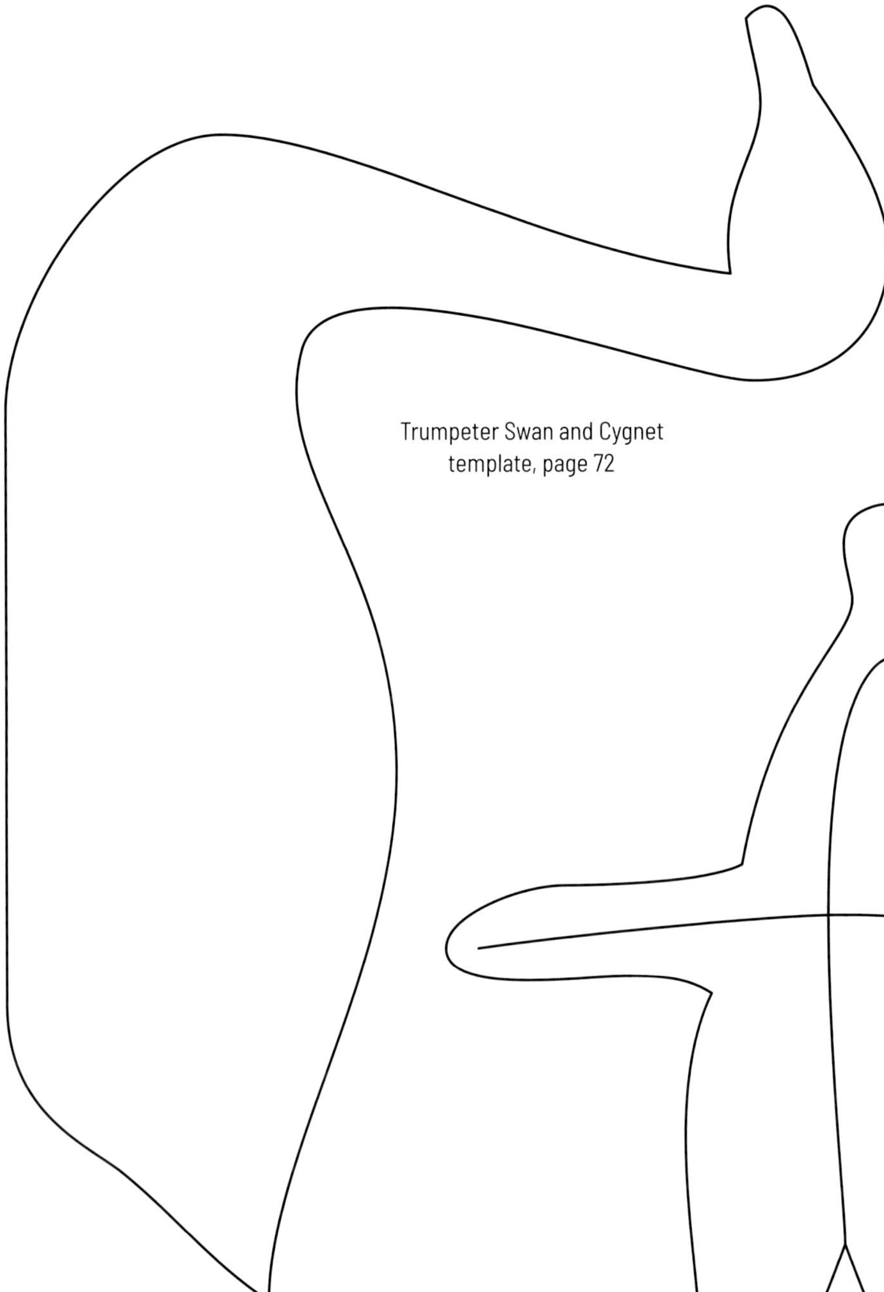

Trumpeter Swan and Cygnet template, page 72

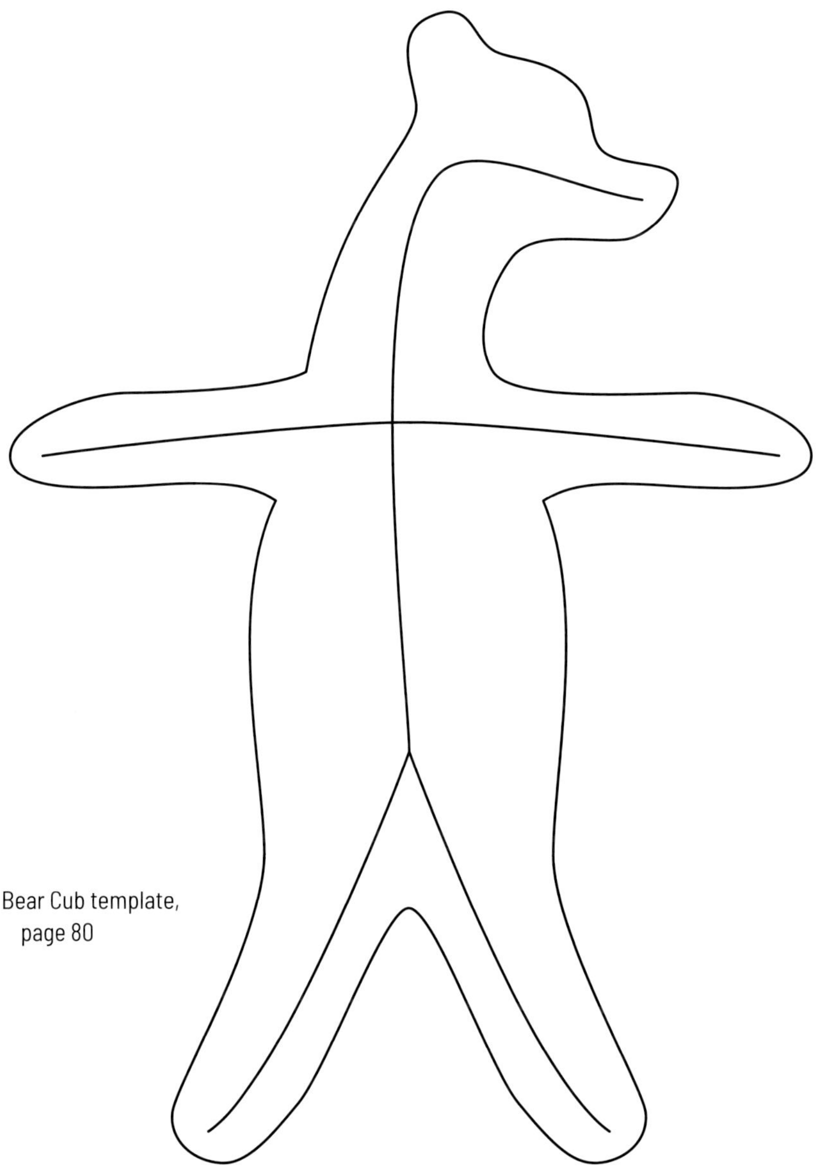

Grizzly Bear Cub template, page 80

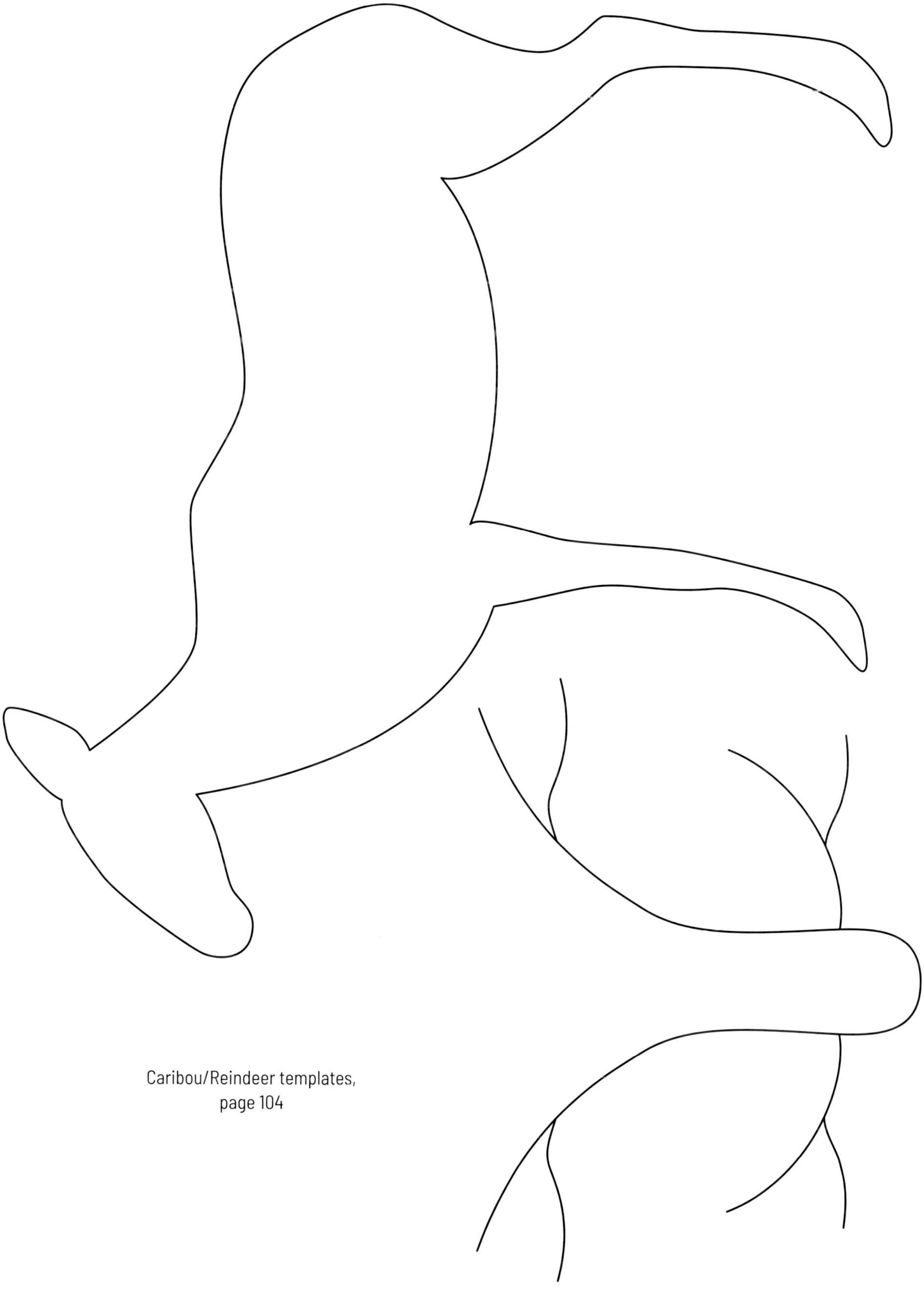

Caribou/Reindeer templates,
page 104

Index

About the Author

Claudia Marie Lenart is a needle felt artist, author, and illustrator. Her wildlife sculptures are realistic, with expressive faces. Her needle-felted animals have a worldwide audience and have been featured in top brand advertising, on TV shows, and in nature museums. Claudia's first how-to book, *Complete Starter Guide to Needle Felting: Enchanted Forest* is among the best sellers in felting books. She also creates nature-inspired wool paintings and has illustrated four children's books using needle felt as her medium. Claudia finds inspiration in the great outdoors and aims to capture the spirit of the animal in her sculptures as she infuses her work with her love and gratitude for the natural world. Claudia's work can be found in her Etsy shop, ClaudiaMarieFelt; on Instagram, @claudiamariefelt; and on her website, *claudiamariefelt.com*.